MAKING SENSE OF HUMOR

HOW TO ADD JOY TO YOUR LIFE

by Lila Green

KiT

Knowledge, Ideas & Trends

Publisher

Manchester, Connecticut

Cover Design: Gil Fahey
Book Design: Cindy Parker

First Published in 1994 by:
Knowledge, Ideas & Trends, Inc.
1131-0 Tolland Turnpike, Suite 175
Manchester, CT 06040
Telephone: 1-800-826-0529

Library of Congress Cataloging-in-Publication Data

Green, Lila.
    Making sense of humor : how to add humor and joy to
your life / by Lila Green.
        p.   cm.
    Includes bibliographical references.
    ISBN 1-897198-12-6 : $10.00
    1. Humor.   2. Conduct of life.   3. Title.
BF575.L7G7   1994
152.4--dc20

                                        94-5527
                                        CIP

10 9 8 7 6 5 4 3 2

First Edition; Second Printing
Printed in the United States of America

DEDICATION

To my parents, Harry and Betty Schlossman, who left me a priceless legacy — love and love of laughter.

To my husband, Bob, who manifested his marvelous sense of humor by marrying me.

To my children, Sue Green Henderson, Carol Green, Janet Green, Dan Green, and Bert Green. Growing up with all five of you was fun — and funny!

And to my grandchildren Erin, Ben and Abby — an endless source of joy, cheer and delight in my life.

Cheerful and grateful thanks to:

Dorothy Coons
Carol Green
Ellen Halter
Charlotte Hanson
Susan Henderson
Pat Materka
Bunny Sandler
Barbra Streisand

and all my other friends who read, made suggestions, and acted as midwives to me to help bring about the birth of this book.

And to my new friends, Rita McCullough and Sandy Brown of KIT Publishing, Inc. How wonderfully wise you both are!

Contents

INTRODUCTION

You probably don't need convincing.

You wouldn't have picked up this book if you hadn't believed, or at least suspected, that humor is one of our most powerful human assets.

Humor is all around us, yet we tend to take it for granted. It occurs naturally and spontaneously. We hear a joke or see something funny and amusement bubbles up inside us, unplanned — although never unwelcome. If humor happens as naturally as sleeping and eating, what more can be said about it?

Plenty!

After all, there are books about how to sleep better, and tens of thousands of cookbooks aimed at eating better. It's high time for a book on how to "humor" yourself.

Humor is too important to be left to chance.

1

This book compiles hundreds of ways to create more humor in all aspects of your life — at work, at home, in your associations with family and friends, in your time by yourself. It presents a smorgasbord of information, tips and practical ideas. Each chapter has something for everyone. We'll talk about:

- ❀ How humor helps people listen, respond to and remember your message.
- ❀ How to use humor to "lighten up" stressful work settings like hospitals and nursing homes.
- ❀ Rarely discussed issues like "gallows humor;" gender differences in humor; humor and sex.
- ❀ How to nurture a sense of humor in your children.

I have tried to integrate what we know about humor with what we can learn from it. The material comes from hundreds of workshops, seminars and keynote addresses I have presented during the past decade. The participants have included managers and administrators, health care professionals, teachers, union leaders, homemakers, retirees, members of the clergy, dairy farmers and funeral directors. Without a doubt, humor strikes a universal chord.

Almost without exception, the evaluations and feedback following these events center on how "extremely practical and useful" the suggestions were. The audiences appreciated the simple and easy techniques I described for incorporating more humor into their lives.

With equal consistency, they kept asking for more. *Making Sense of Humor* is a response to those requests. It combines my own philosophy and ideas with the suggestions of workshop participants, family members, colleagues and friends. It also incorporates real life anecdotes and examples you can adapt to your own experience.

Humor helps us through the hard times and makes the good times better. It enhances communication, enables learning, diffuses anger, promotes productivity and mediates stress. You'll learn how, why and more in the pages that follow.

Chapter One

Understanding Humor

or

Our Sixth Sense

I am fulfilling a long-time goal: to share with you some of my off-center thoughts (and a few inspirations), to stimulate you, to invigorate you and to lighten your outlook.

Please enjoy reading this book. Learn from it and laugh from it. Life is too important to be taken seriously!

How do we define something as seemingly indefinable as humor? If it came in a bottle, we could send it to a laboratory for chemical analysis. The report might provide a few insights:

- ❀ Humor contains no harsh drugs — although it may be habit-forming!

- ❀ Humor is a powerful antidote to stress.

- ❀ Family humor is a strong and enduring substance — often preserved and passed down through many generations.

- ❀ Humor has a glue-like quality that bonds people together.

- ❀ Humor spreads easily.

5

❀ It's colorful, often brassy and vibrant. There's even such a thing as black humor.

❀ It's sometimes tasteless.

❀ It's rich and nourishing — without fat or calories.

Although it is hard to pinpoint what humor is, it's easy to define what it does. Humor is anything that causes pleasant feelings and enjoyment — a greeting card, a child's antics, a marching band. Humor makes us smile, laugh, feel amused or amazed. It alerts our senses and makes us responsive as well as resilient.

Humor is ageless, timeless and always within reach. It can be seen, heard, felt, written or spoken. It may be planned or spontaneous. It is intensely satisfying whether we experience it alone, with another person or with a cast of thousands!

It has a magical quality, uplifting us.

Why Me? Funny You Should Ask!

I feel that my best qualification for being a humor educator comes from being a mother for 178 years, the combined ages of my five children. Raising five children born in the space of eight years offers proof positive that humor and laughter are the world's best coping mechanisms. A spirit of fun and playfulness got us through those busy years and continues to sustain our family through good times and rough times.

But humor around our house didn't start with my generation. I grew up in a large, supportive, extended family in Brooklyn. I owe much to all of them but especially to my father, Harry Schlossman, who had the special ability of making people feel wonderful about themselves. "You have a radiant manner of speaking," he'd tell someone in a casual meeting. And that person would walk away from that conversation feeling radiant.

When my father was hospitalized with a heart attack, my sister and I and other relatives were at his side. All of us, but especially my father, had

always used humor as a coping mechanism. But somehow this large, busy, impersonal hospital did not seem the appropriate place for laughter. Hospitals have few spaces where laughter is encouraged. All of us acted uncharacteristically somber during these visits. I felt a need to do something.

One day I walked in wearing a pair of "Groucho glasses." From that point on his mood lightened. He smiled at me, "Now there's the daughter I used to know!" I left the Groucho glasses with him and he wore them when his doctor came by during his rounds. This gave the doctor permission to laugh and make a lighthearted remark about how he was a cardiologist, not a plastic surgeon! The incident continued to boost my father's spirits every time he retold it.

My father loved people. He was an ideal role model for humor. He taught me about the capacity of humor to connect with other people and enhance human relationships.

I'm happy to take after my father. In my children's early years I tried both naturally and consciously to emulate him. When one of my kids was sad, I might hand him or her a Snickers bar or a Chuckles candy, saying "This might make you laugh or at least snicker or chuckle." At minimum this usually brought forth smiles and giggles which I would gleefully share with my child.

As my children grew into self-sufficient teenagers, I "played around" with humor as a free-lance journalist. I learned belly dancing, enrolled in dog obedience classes, took up downhill skiing and entered a bridge tournament. I described these adventures in George Plimptonesque articles for our local newspaper. One of my best memories is playing drums (at age 41) in a high school rock band. Wearing a long black wig and headband, psychedelic vest and bell bottoms, I looked like Cher impersonating Ringo.

There is much mirth in mediocrity.

I won no medals at any of these endeavors, but I had great fun doing them and writing about them! The experiences also reinforced one of the cornerstone truths about humor: the need to poke fun at yourself. Will Rogers often said, "You grow up the day you have the first real laugh at yourself." Laughing at yourself keeps everything in perspective. It will preserve your sanity, your self-esteem and your personal relationships.

Humor starts from within, but it needn't be kept to yourself! I found a wonderful outlet for humor by becoming a gag writer for a friend who is a prominent national cartoonist. I have a photocopy of the first $25 commission on my cartoon idea that he sold for $100 to Field and Stream!

These snapshots of my life illustrate how we bring together personal experiences which converge into an individual and unique sense of humor. We each of us write our own "humor history," a scrapbook of personal moments. It is shaped by our family upbringing, incidents and anecdotes, influential teachers, friends and acquaintances, as well as people we've never met, like our favorite comedians, writers and cartoonists.

We often think of someone with a sense of humor as someone who makes people laugh. Robin Williams, Erma Bombeck and Charles Shultz clearly have a sense of humor. But you don't have to be a star comedian or a comic artist to enjoy the benefits of laughter. It's just as rewarding to be on the receiving end. People who laugh have as much of a sense of humor as people who make us laugh. You don't have to be naturally funny to have fun.

Whenever I need to refer to a textbook, I also check the index under humor because I am curious to see how the author has related to it. I'm usually disappointed. Humor or, as the Dewey Decimal system codes it, "Wit and Humor," is almost always absent from the index. Not many authors take laughter seriously.

Dictionaries define "a *sense* of humor" as the capacity to understand or appreciate humor. Each of us has this capacity and the lifelong chance to build on it.

8

No Joking Matter

I've never been a joke teller. I can neither remember nor relate jokes well. (Besides, I am married to a wonderful joke teller, and one per family is more than enough!) Instead, my sense of humor relies more on telling funny stories, writing skits, sharing anecdotes, cartoons, quips, toys, games and cheerful activities like costume parties and whimsical gifts. Intentional silliness — even zaniness — best describes my particular brand of humor. I feel that the relationship between humor and jokes is minimal.

I have always loved to laugh. I once read in a book of averages that "the average American laughs 15 times per day." I don't know where they got the statistic, but overachiever that I am, I began counting how many more times than 15 I laughed each day, determined to beat the norm.

Funny television shows and movies have always appealed to me. They create easy opportunities for laughter. But the idea that humor went beyond the world of entertainment didn't become clear to me until I began working for the University of Michigan Institute of Gerontology. Part of my job involved visiting nursing homes to conduct staff training sessions. It was sad for me to see that there were few opportunities for laughter in these settings, either for the nursing home residents themselves, for the staff or in their interactions with one another.

In a special residential unit for elderly persons with Alzheimer's disease, I was fascinated to observe that residents who could not remember the names of their spouses or children could often tell jokes or long funny stories or sing silly old songs from beginning to end. They enjoyed making humorous remarks and clearly got enormous pleasure from provoking laughter. Of course, the pleasure was mutual. Humor has a powerful bonding effect.

One particularly gloomy day, a mother and two small children came to visit a relative in the Alzheimer's unit. The mother had brought several brightly colored balloons. Soon after their arrival, the children and the residents who were gathered in the lounge began a lively game of balloon tossing. The children giggled and laughed as they chased the balloons and tossed them back and forth among the older people seated about the room. The staff also quickly caught up and joined in the spirit of fun and playfulness.

9

The cheerful mood of that morning lingered long after the children had gone. The incident illustrates perfectly that humor doesn't require fancy props or careful planning.

It also shows how, long after a humorous event takes place, the emotional memory lives on. The good feelings and sense of relaxation cast a brighter color on the day, sometimes for days to come.

Shared laughter is like throwing open the shutters in a gloomy room and letting in fresh air and sunshine.

Laughter is life affirming, at any age and under any circumstance.

What's So Funny?

Having claimed that humor cannot be easily defined or dissected, we will now dauntlessly forge forward and try to figure it out anyway.

Even though different people laugh at different things under different circumstances, researchers have narrowed down some common patterns that make us laugh or amuse us. As you review them, think about how each of these relates to such different forms of humor as vaudeville, television sitcoms, movies, books, cartoons and comic strips.

Surprise — The slapstick slip on a banana

peel, the pratfall or the pie-in-the-face all illustrate surprise. Jokes frequently have the element of surprise. You expect one logical ending to a story, and then a new twist — the illogical or unexpected punch line causes laughter. Some of the funniest — and most memorable and effective — television commercials deliver their message with a quirky surprise.

Exaggeration — Picture a clown — better yet, a tiny truckload of clowns, skittering across the sawdust into the center ring of the circus. A dozen of them are crowded into a toy-sized fire engine. They circle around and then tumble out, wearing hats the size of teacups or shoes as big as skateboards. Exaggerating things out of proportion tickles our funny bone.

Caricatures, like clowns, are another example of visual exaggeration. We get pleasure from exaggerated *tastes* like spicy five-alarm chili or double fudge ice cream, and from the sensation of exaggerated *sounds* like the boom of cannons at the finale of the 1812 Overture.

Here are some other examples of humor in exaggeration:

❀ A cupcake with 40 birthday candles

❀ Christmas tree ornaments worn as earrings

❀ A life-sized teddy bear in the office of a college president

❀ A $100 bill printed the size of a theater ticket (so you can truthfully claim "the smallest bill I have is a hundred.")

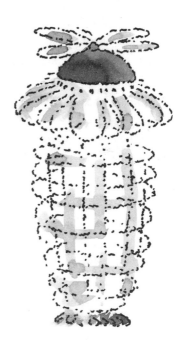

Reversal — Like surprise and exaggeration, reversal catches us off guard and offers us a fresh way of looking at things, a new perspective. Reversal means we expect one thing and the opposite occurs. It also includes incongruities: in the Peanuts comic strip, children speak like sophisticated adults; in Gary Larson's "Far Side," animals behave more intelligently than humans. The Three Stooges are grown men who act like children. Some other examples of incongruity or reversal are:

❀ Mismatched pairs like Mutt and Jeff; Laurel and Hardy.

❀ An indoor beach party in January.

❀ Wearing a shoe on your head.

❀ Eating dessert first.

Teachers can use reversal to help students better understand a learning concept. For example, instead of lecturing on the best ways to study for a test, she could ask students for examples of how not to study — i.e., turn on the television, don't take notes, etc.

When our expectations aren't met, we may be disappointed but we often react with delight. Want to try it on yourself? The next time you get into the bathtub, sit facing away from the faucet. Or face your fellow passengers instead of the door on your next elevator journey.

Humor reminds us that there's room for flexibility in our world. Because it is fraught with surprises, reversals and unexpected twists, humor gives us the chance to step back from our assumptions with a lightness and openness.

Take for example the case of the woman standing at a bus stop next to a dog. A man walks up to her and asks if her dog bites.

"No," she replies. The man pets the dog and in return gets a big bite on the leg.

Astonished, the man turns to the woman and says, "I thought you said your dog doesn't bite!"

The woman replies, "That's not my dog."

Some Four-Letter Words

In my humor workshops I play with four large cut-out letters — two H's

12

and two A's. Spelled **HA HA** they help illustrate the connection between laughter, learning and healthful living. HA HA represents Humor Awareness / Humor Attitude.

Building on the concept of awareness, I move the letters around to spell **AH HA!** to illustrate the power of humor as an educational tool to gain attention, to make people more receptive to learning, and to help them remember what they learned.

Finally, I shift the letters to spell **AAHH!** Humor may be the best stress reliever there is. If you have ever laughed so hard that you doubled over, fell off your chair, spit out food or wet your pants, you've had this experience. You cannot maintain muscle tension when you are laughing.

So, to return to the original topic of "What is humor?" we can conclude that among all its magical qualities, one of its greatest values is as an antidote to stress. According to William James, "We do not laugh because we are happy . . . we are happy because we laugh." In an increasingly high-pressured and unpredictable world, we need a stress reliever that requires no prescription and has no bad side effects. And if it's habit forming, so much the better!

One of the biggest barriers to humor development is the belief that it's something you're born with. Either you've "got it" and you're lucky, or you "haven't got it," and, poor thing, you never will. Some people resist trying humor on for size because they are afraid of appearing foolish. They want others to know that they take life seriously!

I agree with Joel Goodman, director of the Humor Project, who calls humor "a set of skills, attitudes and guidelines that we can consciously access. Like any set of skills, humor can be nurtured through practice."

This is as far as we need to go in analyzing humor because, as Mark Twain said,

"When you dissect a frog, you learn a lot about the frog. But you end up with a dead frog."

The purpose of this book is not to analyze humor to death, but to bring it to life!

Especially to your life!

CHAPTER TWO

HUMOR AND COMMUNICATION

OR

MIRTH IN YOUR MESSAGE

The invitation has been on your refrigerator for weeks. You are wearing a new outfit and have bought flowers for the hostess. Your anticipation is high. Yes! Some social events are a drag, but you've been looking forward to this one.

You arrive, size up the room and head for a lively-looking group around the living room sofa. Antennae raised, you quickly tune in on the conversations:

"…married 26 years and he ran off with his dental hygienist. The kids? Oh yes, devastated…"

"…bankrupt. You could have fooled me. I thought they were rolling in money…"

"…rain every day from the moment we arrived until our departure. And the temperatures were about 20 degrees below normal…"

Have you been to this party? Do you know these people?

We work with them, we live with them, we like them, yet often we talk with them about the gloomiest things! Heavy traffic, high cholesterol, rising taxes. Disease of the week. Divorce of the month. Sigh, groan, grimace. Isn't it awful? What's the world coming to?

Can we please lighten up? Can we add some mirth to our message?

Conversations like these rarely solve problems; they just leave us drained and debilitated. We can't avoid bad news, but we won't change it by dwelling on it.

Good news, on the other hand, tends to boost our energy level as it lifts our spirits. Even if the pessimist is sometimes right in the long run, it's the optimist who has more fun on the trip.

Communication is one vehicle for putting more humor in your life. You have a way with words.

Words Words Words…

"…I'm so sick of words," sang Eliza Doolittle. After all those grueling hours with Henry Higgins she well knew the power they held. They begin as harmless groups of letters, abcdefghijklmnopqrstuvwxyz. Strung together to form sentences, they can be hammered into opinions and ideas. They can alter our view of the world.

Like air into a balloon, words have the power to:

❀ Inflate ("That was an excellent proposal you submitted." "That haircut makes you look wonderful!") or

❀ Deflate ("Can't you ever remember to refill the gas tank?" "Putting on a little weight there, aren't you?")

Inflating words pay a compliment, share a funny story, draw a positive comparison, recreate a happy memory, entertain, amuse, motivate.

Deflating words criticize, express doubt, withdraw support, lament, ridicule, frighten, belittle, anger, alienate.

A reminder that bears repeating: as you build your humor vocabulary, steer clear of words that are ethnically biased, sexist, ageist or racist. Good words connect people; they never exclude or offend.

Keep your message in good taste. You never know when you may have to eat your words!

A Picture is Worth A Thousand

Words, spoken and written, form the basis of communication. But communication can also be shared laughter, a wink, a touch, a hug. Cartoons communicate humor. So does a whimsical necktie or earrings, a windup toy or a smile.

Borrowing from the dictionary, we may define humor in communication as: "The ability to perceive, enjoy or express what is comical or funny." (American Heritage Dictionary)

"That which causes pleasant feelings and enjoyment, causing reactions of smiling, laughing or feelings of amusement." (Webster's New World Dictionary)

Both define humor as a two-way process. It's both:

❀ how we convey information to others, and

❀   how we interpret the information that comes to us.

You may be the sender or the receiver of these pleasant feelings. In the best of all situations, you can be both! Spreading humor is like blowing a mature dandelion against the wind. It floats right back to you.

Different Jokes for Different Folks

Humor in communication means much more than telling jokes. You don't have to become a stand-up comic or practice punch lines to raise your **HA HA** (Humor Awareness Humor Attitude) level. Communicated humor can be:

❀   Verbal — witty sayings, wisecracks, puns, parody, funny stories, anecdotes, sarcasm, satire, jokes, jests, or

❀   Visual — cartoons, comics, toys, gags, comedy, slapstick, clowning, pantomime, signs, funny clothes, costumes.

This amazing resource can be seen, spoken, heard, held, read, written or worn! It can even be purchased at a toy or gift shop! But mostly it is free of charge because it comes from within.

Humor is not necessarily a funny punchline or a rubber nose. It is not "something" but "somehow." It is the ability to find humor in every day frustrations and inconveniences like long grocery lines and endless games of telephone tag. More, it's the knack for turning these adversities to your advantage. Instead of fuming in the checkout line, you can read the National Enquirer cover to cover. "Chocoholic Mother Gives Birth To Sugar-Coated Baby!" How else would you have known?!

Cultivate an *appreciation* — rather than a mere tolerance — for the absurdities and incongruities of life.

Look for humor and it will find you. And don't forget to look in the mirror. One of the most positive traits you can develop is the ability to laugh at yourself.

From Ha Ha to Ah Ha!

Why are the color comics wrapped around the Sunday newspaper? Why do most keynote speakers start off with a joke?

Because humor gets our attention! It grabs us by the collar and makes us more alert and receptive to the information to follow.

Communication conveys information and ideas. It has the power to educate, enlighten, motivate and inspire. It connects you with another individual — or legions of them. Humor smoothes the path.

You can weigh your message down with a somber tone and furrowed brow — "this is serious, folks" — and risk scaring or boring them to death. Or you can spice it with humor and win them over instantly.

"Wit is the salt of conversation," says British essayist William Hazlitt.

The applications are numerous:

Education: Humor creates a lively and stimulating learning environment, "humanizes" the teacher and decreases discipline problems. A group of fifth graders decided that at a given signal, they would all push their books off their desks. Around mid-morning while the teacher was turned to the blackboard, the signal was given and books from each desk crashed to the floor. The teacher wheeled around to face the giggling class, collected her thoughts, and then knocked the books off her desk as well. "Sorry I was late," she said. Her quick response showed she appreciated their humor.

Sales: The marketing brochure, magazine ad or television commercial that makes us smile is more likely to hold our attention. We're more apt to remember the product and feel positive about it.

Humor can help people in sales remain cool and confident in the ever-present face of rejection. Have you heard the one about the traveling salesman whose product broke down during the demonstration? Thinking fast, he told the customer, "That was our competitor's version!"

Management: Studies show that employees who have fun at work are more creative and productive. Absenteeism and turnover are lower, and morale improves in a more playful work environment.

A staff meeting was called to discuss the consequences of a severe sales slump. Each employee was charged to submit an idea for reducing the upcoming annual budget. One of the district managers came up with a novel solution. She took the ledger from the annual report, and reduced it on the copy machine to the size of a postage stamp. Her "solution" caused laughter, reduced tension, and led to a productive problem-solving discussion.

Health care: Humor reduces the inevitable stress in hospitals, clinics and long-term care facilities. It builds rapport among staff and between staff and patients and may even play a role in the patient's recovery.

A staff member of an extended care unit noticed that one of the residents had her blouse buttoned on backwards. She tactfully called it to the woman's attention. "That's okay," the patient replied wryly. "These days I don't know if I'm coming or going!" The two shared a hearty laugh that made them feel closer to each other.

Politics: Humor creates rapport between candidate and constituency. It can be used to illustrate and reinforce where she or he stands on the issues.

Ronald Reagan was a master at it, even after he was shot by a sniper in 1981. He looked at the medical team and asked, "I hope you surgeons are all Republicans?!"

Breaking the Ice

If you enjoy music, you don't sit around waiting for a brass band to march past your window. You turn on the radio. You *plan* for ways to bring music into your life.

Humor can be planned and provided for as well. Many people overlook this possiblity. Since surprise is one of the key elements of humor, they assume that humor is always spontaneous.

Nonsense. Humor is entirely too important to be left to chance.

As a professional speaker, I've learned that one must be prepared to be funny. Expect disasters! When the lights black out in the middle of your talk, "Would someone please inform the electric company that the check is in the mail?" Or, "Now we'll talk for a moment about black humor...."

Here are some easy ways to communicate more humor to yourself and those around you:

- ❀ Collect cartoons and jokes to post on the bulletin board or share with your friends.
- ❀ Create a humorous motto for yourself; for example: Ashleigh Brilliant's book title, "I may not be perfect, but parts of me are excellent!"
- ❀ Collect silly and ridiculous gifts for your friends, and don't wait for a special occasion to give them.
- ❀ Practice retelling a joke five times the same day you hear it.
- ❀ Hang out with people who laugh and find joy in their lives.

Finally, be that person who finds joy in your life. You only need to look for it. Make time for your favorite TV comedy show. Clip cartoons from the newspaper or magazine. Watch children at play. Stroke a kitten or puppy. And share these experiences with the people with whom you live and work. Greet the receptionist in the morning with a cheerful observation, not a gripe about the parking shortage.

At a loss for words? Perhaps you're visiting your grandparents, searching your mind for an upbeat, innovative question that can move the conversation past ailments and regrets. How about: if it's your grandmother, "What was the prettiest dress you ever wore?" And Grandpa will love to respond to this: "Tell me about your first car!" Often these questions will lead to humorous anecdotes and generate smiles.

Here are some more conversation starters to keep talk on a positive note. Use them when visiting someone in the hospital or as an icebreaker at the next family reunion:

- ❀ "What were some of your favorite toys and games when you were growing up?"

21

❀ "Who's your favorite comedian?"

❀ "Who makes you laugh more than anyone else you know?"

❀ "Where would you pick to go on your dream vacation?"

❀ "If you could be a little kid for a day, how would you spend your day?"

❀ "If a movie were going to be made of your life, which actor or actress would you pick to portray you? Who would you consider the worst person to portray you?"

❀ "If you were to be described as an animal, which one would you be?"

❀ "If you could write your own fortune cookie, what message would you convey?"

❀ "If you had $1 million to give to any group or cause, to whom would you give it and why?"

❀ "What's the best advice you've ever been given?"

❀ "What's the [strangest, funniest, worst, best] thing you've ever done for money?"

❀ "If people were in zoos, which group and types would be the most popular for the animals to come watch?"

❀ "If you were to write your autobiography, what would the title be?"

❀ "Tell me about one of the happiest days of your life."

In Summary

Humor in communication serves to:

❀ Gain attention

❀ Build rapport with your listener

❀ Stimulate creativity and problem-solving

❀ Defuse tension and conflict

❀ Illustrate a point in a memorable way

❀ Make bad news more palatable

❀ Reinforce the message

❀ Provide a "memory hook" for remembering

Victor Borge said, "Laughter is the shortest distance between two people." Humor and laughter create a bond that facilitates communication and strengthens relationships.

What could be more important?

Chapter Three

Humor and Family and Friends

or

Familiarity Breeds Content

"Who makes you laugh or smile?"

I ask this question in my humor workshops — or *play*shops — to illustrate that each of us reacts to humor in an individual way. One person cracks up at the Three Stooges' slapstick; another finds them unbearable. People mention Joan Rivers, Bill Cosby, Charlie Chaplan or Erma Bombeck. Each has a different style, but a huge following. Each strikes a different chord or a different funny bone.

So we go around the room, each person naming a favorite comedian, writer or cartoon character. And then someone says, "My son Ben makes me laugh," or "My best friend Evelyn," and we are reminded of another whole wonderful category of human humor resources, often right under our roof — our families and friends.

Extended Families

These days, the word family may refer to a much more complex social unit than Mom, Dad and their 2.3 children. Divorce and remarriage have led to blended and extended families. A child has only one biological mother and father but may have any number of stepparents, stepbrothers or sisters, half brothers or sisters, and grandparents, aunts, uncles and cousins of various lineage. Family implies multiple generations.

We are seeing the emergence of multi-ethnic families due to intermarriage, interracial adoption, and adoption of children from foreign countries.

At the smaller end of the spectrum, the single parent with a child is a family. So are gay/lesbian couples, many of whom are raising kids.

Finally, for single people in particular but many of the rest of us as well, friends and co-workers also constitute family. We spend more time with our office mates than our housemates. We celebrate each other's birthdays, collaborate on important projects and share confidences. Common interests and day-to-day experiences create this sense of family.

All of this underscores a congenial blurring of the lines between family and friends. Switch on the television. On the classic I Love Lucy show, the Ricardos and the Mertzes were family. The medical staff in M*A*S*H were family. Ozzie & Harriet and the boys were a traditional family, but the Brady

26

Bunch and the bar room gang on Cheers fit our definition as well.

The common denominator is caring, not kinship.

Humor Begins in Childhood

The most critical element in personal development is self-esteem. It forms the basis for other kinds of mastery — from our ability to engage in work to our success in social relationships.

Humor is integral to the development of self-esteem. Through humor and playfulness, children get a chance to practice other intellectual and social skills. They say something funny and people smile or laugh. Humor enhances self-esteem because being liked by others leads us to like ourselves.

And the payoffs are similar to those experienced by adults. Humor:

- ❀ invites interaction
- ❀ puts others at ease
- ❀ wins affection
- ❀ helps in coping with fear and stress.

"It's difficult not to like someone who makes you laugh," says Dr. Paul E. McGhee, author of *Humor and Children's Development: A Guide to Practical Applications.* Research with preschool and elementary school children shows that children who initiate jokes and humor are more popular with adults and playmates.

McGhee identifies five stages in the development of childhood humor:

I. Infancy: silly sounds and funny faces

Infants have the ability to smile almost from birth. "It's only gas," the nurse may tell us, but even in that context we can see that a smile is a natural release of tension. Within a few months, a baby smiles readily in response to funny faces and smiles. As babies approach their first birthday, they giggle and laugh when Daddy barks like a dog or wears a shoe on his head.

II. Toddlers: pratfalls and slapstick

27

In learning to crawl, walk and climb, toddlers explore the world through their actions. Tumbling and crashing into obstacles is as likely to make them laugh as cry. As they begin to understand the functions of objects, they also find humor in scrambling them — like wearing socks as mittens or pretending spaghetti is worms.

III. Preschoolers: joke telling

"Knock knock." "Who's there?" The rest of it hardly matters because, during the three-to-five year stage, what children love most is the process of joke-telling more than the content. Eager to practice their language skills, they love to be the center of attention and they love to make their audience laugh.

Bathroom humor emerges at this stage. Why? Because on the heels of toilet training, young children are sensitive to the social embarrassment of having an accident. "Pee-pee" jokes help them cope with this tension.

IV. Elementary school — riddles and puns

As the child's verbal skills continue to grow, words with double meanings become a popular form of humor. Sight gags and slapstick still have their place, but by now children find special delight in surprising their audience with a play on words or a twist ending. "Why is tennis the loudest sport?" "Because all the players raise a racket."

V. Adolescence — situation comedy

By high school, teenagers' humor is merging with that of adults. Formula jokes and riddles have given way to spontaneous wit and plays on words. Teasing and put-downs, including self-deprecating humor, is commonplace.

Ethnic, racist and sexist forms of humor often emerge at this time. This poses a dilemma for parents. If you laugh, you're telling them such jokes are acceptable. If you forbid them to use such humor, they may be even more likely to share the jokes with their peers.

When your teenager makes a joke that you think is hurtful or inappropriate, use it as an opportunity to discuss harmful stereotypes. Part of growing up and gaining self-esteem is learning that it is not gained at the expense of others.

Question: Should women have children after thirty-five?

Answer: No, thirty-five children are enough!

As The Twig Is Bent

At each of the preceding stages, humor is important to a child's personal development. Think about your own upbringing. What role did laughter play in your family while you were growing up? Was each day greeted as a gift, or grimly regarded as something to "get through"? Did your parents encourage silliness, or did they foster the notion that "life is serious"?

I believe humor is the one thing we should take seriously.

I come from a family of laughter. My parents weren't rich, and neither were my uncles, aunts and dozens of cousins growing up in post-Depression Brooklyn. But there was plenty of merriment, especially on Sunday evenings when we gathered at the big round table at my aunt's house across the street. The relatives told stories about one another. They laughed into the night about all the things that had gone wrong. The unspoken punch line was, "...and we *survived!*"

By the late 1940s, an aunt had bought a television, the first on the block. I remember how we would gather in her tiny living room on Tuesday nights, ready to laugh with "Uncle Miltie." Milton Berle brought us together for the purpose of laughing. This is another example of creating joyful occasions, getting people together, and planning to laugh.

My husband Bob and I have tried to pass on this heritage of shared laughter to our five children. (This was not difficult since raising five children, in itself, takes a sense of humor!) Along with other values, such as courtesy, honesty and self-respect, we have tried to nurture the value of fun and playfulness.

Here are a few suggestions from the collective experience of the Green family and others:

Don't practice mirth control

Messages such as "Wipe that smile off your face!" and "Why don't you act your age?" tell our kids that life is serious and playfulness is ill-mannered and wrong. Teach your children to recognize unkind and inappropriate humor, but don't turn them against lightheartedness.

Lighten up the meals

This doesn't refer to the calorie count. Mealtime is often the only time the entire family gathers so make a rule against bickering, complaining and scolding. Take turns telling a joke or riddle or a funny thing that happened that day.

It's been said that "a heavy heart is the most serious form of overweightedness." Humor may be the ultimate diet!

Create family rituals

As you'll recall from Chapter One, two key sources of humor are reversal and exaggeration. We use them in some of our favorite family rituals:

Staying Up All Night — The kids often begged to stay up all night during the summer so once a year we complied. We'd camp out in the living room, eat popcorn and tell stories. They knew if they dozed off, however, they would be shaken and wakened and forced to watch another video. No one was permitted to sleep until sun up.

Dessert first dinners — We eat dessert as a first course and then the main dish. These once-a-month rituals are now carried on by my adult children for our grandchildren.

Reverse child/parent roles — One night a week let kids get parents off to bed by reading to them, supervising tooth brushing, singing a lullaby and tucking in bed.

Family portraits with Groucho glasses — Everyone who sees these photos marvels at the family resemblance!

Family Talent Shows — Or Everyone Gets into the Act — Plan to showcase each family member by holding Talent Shows at family gatherings. Watching and listening to Grandma recite a familiar poem from her childhood days or seeing a favorite Uncle dramatically re-enact *Casey at the Bat*, permits a lighthearted side to relatives. Everyone likes to shine in the spotlight!

Let kids plan a wedding ceremony and reception to celebrate their parent's wedding anniversary.

Create a ritual for stress relief

Find a wild, outlandish activity in which everyone in the family can participate. Once while using a hot air popcorn popper, I forgot to position a bowl under the spout. The popcorn flew all over the kitchen counter, chairs, table and floor. It was a hilarious sight! We all burst out laughing, and we now have a new stress reliever — a popcorn explosion party!

Invent playful names

My son Bert became "Smedley, the butler" when it was his turn to do unpleasant chores. Your daughter could be "Hortensia, the maid."

Make choretime musical

Put on a Sousa march and put some pep into the housework! Let your older children and teenagers play their rock records at full volume for these "special" occasions.

Music makes household tasks funishment, not punishment.

Set complaints to music

The next time you hear, "Tommy won't let me play with his truck," ask your child to sing the complaint. The sour notes will soon dissolve into giggles.

Leave notes from inanimate objects.

"Please hang me up. Love, your towel," is a nicer form of nagging and more likely to be remembered. Look for other unexpected places to leave a cartoon or a surprise message — on a pillow, in a suitcase, in a lunch box.

Keep a prop box

Use it to store crazy hats, Groucho glasses, a feather boa, masks, toys and other gimmicks that need not be reserved for Halloween. Ours also contains a toy magic wand. When a family member does something nice for another — like folding the laundry or setting the table — the magic wand is left as a signature. Now it's the recipient's turn to re-place the wand after returning the favor.

Start a humor scrapbook for your child

A two-year-old can make a funny drawing or point out funny pictures in magazines for you to clip and save. Older children can collect cartoons, jokes and riddles and watch their humor sense grow like the cents in their piggy banks. This activity starts children on the worthwhile course of looking for humor and appreciating its value.

Keep a family humor journal

More than a scrapbook, this includes a record of funny quotes and anecdotes along with the traditional snapshots and mementos of family events. It can also preserve cartoons after their time on the refrigerator door is up. Family humor books can be reviewed and added to on holidays and at family reunions in years to come.

Merry Monthly Mail

I address five envelopes at the beginning of every month, one to each member of my family, who live all over the country. During the month, as I read newspapers and magazines, I clip out cartoons, articles, anecdotes and pictures and place them in the envelope for the appropriate person. At the end of the month I write a group letter. My envelope is already filled with light-hearted thoughts. Sometimes, I receive the same cartoon from one of my family in the mail—reinforcing that we are on the same humor wave length!

Look back with laughter

Tell and re-tell stories about events that were not funny at the time. Embarrassing or upsetting incidents often become family treasure tales as time passes. Kids love to hear stories about Mom or Dad or other family members getting in and out of tricky situations — and surviving. The ability to laugh at past mistakes or misfortunes is worth passing on to our children.

PLAY!

Lose your stuffiness! Go roller skating. Jump in the leaf pile. Roll down a hill. Have a flapjack flipping contest. Make funny faces. Build a sand castle at the beach. Start a snowball fight. Hold a family talent show.

Don't Postpone Joy

Children are masters at play. They can learn to use a computer, solve Rubik's cube and assemble other puzzles more quickly than many adults. They approach the task as play. Life is a smorgasbord of adventure and delightful discoveries.

Adults, on the other hand, often approach a task with a sense of duty and resignation. We want to do it fast, do it well, and get it over with. This means "getting serious" — putting more pressure on ourselves.

Children experience the joy of life — and parents can share this if we let them set the pace.

Sometimes busy parents are so rushed and anxious to cross "To Do" items off lists, they forget to add "Play" to their long lists. Sue, a busy and creative mother, tells about a happy event with her three year old. The two of them had come out of a movie bargain matinee at dusk just as it was starting to rain. Sue looked at her daughter and said, "Abby, I'd like to teach you to sing and dance in the rain." Abby said, "Okay, Mommy." The two of them played in the deserted parking lot in the rain, holding hands and skipping for about 20 minutes. Sue claims that this was a very special time

Time flies—whether you're having fun or not!

ᴇr driving her 12 year old home from a piano lesson notices ᴛʜᴀᴛ   ᴇr is enjoying a song on the radio. As they reach their driveway, aware that the song is not yet over, the mother drives around the block until the song ends.

We stuff each day with serious endeavors, conscientiously recording our tasks and goals on a daily To Do list and crossing off each accomplishment. Sometimes we are more attuned to the things left on our list than what we've so far accomplished!

I'd like you to pause for a moment. Grab a pencil and a sheet of paper, and make another list. (Do it now! No fair procrastinating.) First, write down 10 things you really enjoy doing. Your "love to do" list can include anything from quick to complicated, from sipping a milk shake to backpacking through the High Sierras.

Now, next to each item, write the date of the *last time* you did each of the items on your list.

Workshop participants who do this exercise are astonished and sad to discover how infrequently they permit themselves to do the things they enjoy most! What are we waiting for? Life is not a dress rehearsal!

Starting today, promise yourself you'll make a habit of doing something good for yourself as regularly as you brush your teeth!

On weekends, holidays and days off, create a "Not To Do List."

And next New Year's Eve, make a resolution to "Pursue Pleasure." Forget cleaning the files and losing 10 pounds. Give those a rest. Instead, resolve to

Play more
Act silly
Be happy.

Fun and Friendship

"Hello Timmy. Can your mommy and daddy come out to play?"

Picture this — the couple next door waiting eagerly outside on your porch perhaps holding a bat and catcher's mitt. Alas, our lives are too busy for this frivolity. Don't they know we're busy??! Few of us feel free to drop whatever we're doing to join an impromptu neighborhood game of softball or hide and seek.

But even grownups recognize the value of reserving time to play with friends. We plan business lunches and business meetings. Shouldn't we plan play lunches and play meetings as well?

Plan is the key word here. It could mean:
- ❀ Inviting the neighbors over for dessert cheer
- ❀ Hosting an evening of Charades, Pictionary or Trivial Pursuit
- ❀ Signing up for ballroom dance lessons
- ❀ Organizing *any* group activity, whether it's cross-country skiing, a holiday sing-along, a progressive dinner — you name it.

A group of my women friends decided several years ago to take tap dancing lessons. Wonderful mortar for cementing friendships! We called ourselves the MADAMS, for "Middle-Aged Dancers Are Marvelous!" Later, we became the Women's Primarily (Prime Merrily), so-called because we were not the Women's *Auxiliary* of anything!

Now when our group gets together, we *plan to play*. We have potluck suppers and share potluck feelings. We play children's games like jacks and pick-up sticks. We recite all the rhymes to children's jump rope songs we can remember.

Humor and fun deserve such a prominent place in our lives. Some people hesitate to reveal the lighter side of their nature for fear of looking foolish. On the contrary, playfulness communicates confidence. Professional speakers who can weave a funny story into a serious message show the audience they are in control. The same goes for expressing humor in other areas of our personal and professional relationships.

We all have friends that we can be serious with, but I think a *really* great friend is one we can be silly with.

Many of us have to deal with difficult people. Ed, a busy stockbroker re-frames the situation when it's his turn with difficult individuals. He thinks, "Three percent of all people in the world are put here to irritate us. You, difficult

35

person, are just doing your job. And you're very good at it!"

Allowing ourselves to be playful and silly does not undermine our dignity. If anything, it enhances our authority by helping us build rapport with others.

Teachable Skills

"My husband (or wife, or boss, or friend) has no sense of humor. How can I get him or her to lighten up?" Someone once described her boss as having had a "charisma bypass!"

I'm asked this question more than any other. I am sorry to say the answer appears to be, you can't. We can't instill a sense of humor in another adult any more than we can instill a conscience. A sense of humor is an attitude toward life — one that doesn't let you take yourself too seriously. I am not a therapist, but I believe you cannot change someone's personality. Change has to come from within. However, I do believe we can foster a sense of fun and playfulness in our children. And we can create an environment for our friends and our families that invites laughter. We can model cheerful attitudes. In creating a playful, fun environment for ourselves, we may influence them to join in. A joyous approach to life increases your sense of self mirth! More about that in the CELEBRATIONS chapter coming up next!

You and You Alone

For people who live alone, a dog, cat or other pet can offer a high-spirited source of playfulness that is irresistible and irreplaceable. And if owning a pet is not realistic at this time, create an opportunity to watch children at play. Go to a park. Visit a zoo or a playground. Observing a child is almost certain to bring you a smile or a chuckle, and will keep you in touch with the child within you.

Seek out positive people. But most of all enjoy yourself. The only person guaranteed to be with you all your life is you — so make sure you enjoy your own company. Find out what tickles you and incorporate more of those things into your life.

36

Some final reminders:

- ❀ Create special lighthearted occasions (like the family dinner hour or your favorite TV comedy) to share with family and friends.
- ❀ Laugh *with* other people, not at them. Avoid put-down humor, and never make jokes at a child's expense.
- ❀ Give yourself permission to be silly, dramatic or playful. When my three-year-old grandson and I play hide and seek, he doesn't ask me, "Why are we doing this?" We are playing for the sake of play and it feels wonderful!
- ❀ Use exaggeration to put worries in perspective. ("What's the worst thing that could happen?")
- ❀ *Plan* to play.
- ❀ Remember, the best things in life aren't *things.*
- ❀ It's been said, "Laughter is like changing a baby's diaper. It may not solve the problem permanently, but it surely improves the situation for the moment!"

And: it's also been said: after love, the next best thing you can leave your family and friends is a legacy of laughter.

TLC — Time for Laughter and Cheer

Parents — laugh at your own mistakes! This will show children how to use humor to handle difficulties.

Singing is one of the easiest ways for families to enjoy each other's creativity and silliness. Very small children and their parents have fun by singing nursery rhymes. Others enjoy sound effect songs such as Old MacDonald or action songs such as John Brown's Baby. Rounds offer opportunities for developing unity and teamwork playfully. Singing in harmony (or trying to) may lead to laughter. "Create a Song" on long car trips. Select one person to be "singer." This person chooses a letter of the alphabet and all other participants name a word beginning with that chosen letter. The designated singer has to create a song using all the words named.

Exaggerate — have fun with excuses. Encourage children to come up with clever excuses such as "I didn't do the dishes...because there were sharks in the sink."

Celebrate Valentine's Day with a Heart's Desire Dinner — Everyone gets to eat what he wants to — no lectures — no guilt. Sample menu: sugar cereal and candy.

Cartoons — Place a cartoon in your kid's lunchbox — or your wife's briefcase. Create space on one kitchen cupboard for cartoons. Cut off the caption from a cartoon and pass it around at dinner asking all present to come up with a caption of their own.

Five senses — plus sense of humor plus nonsense.

Children are not born whimsically impaired!

Sense of humor is a powerful magnet for friendship (life's most important treasure).

When our children are little, we spend enormous energy and time (ever watch grandparents making silly faces at their newborn grandchild?) encouraging smiles and laughter from babies. What happens when the child gets older? Some messages may be: "Wipe that smile off your face!" or "This is not laughing matter!" or "We have no time for silliness!!" or "Act your age!!!! You're a big girl/boy now!"

My neighbor, Molly, has a group of friends who have been getting together for lunches every Friday afternoon for over 40 years. These women all worked together establishing a Planned Parenthood organization. Their luncheon is called "Friday Friends." Hostessing this event is on a rotating basis. The hostess provides dessert, coffee and tea. Each guest arrives carrying her own sandwich. The lack of work required for gatherings of this type make it easy to continue. The women have been a support group for each other, crying and laughing together at the changes in their lives. Sharing, food, friendship and fun has been deeply important and meaningful to this group.

Erma Bombeck doesn't lead a funnier life than most of us. She just sees the humor in everyday situations and has the marvelous gift of being able to write about family situations from her own delightful perspective. Think about how Erma Bombeck might write a column about your family.

Don't sweat the small stuff...it's all small stuff!

Laughter is like sunshine in a home — it brightens everything!

Parenting is too important to be taken seriously!

Encourage attempts at children's humor by laughing easily and heartily (even if you've heard the joke, pun or riddle hundreds of times!). Laughing *with* children enhances self-esteem. Once your child experiences the wonderful feeling of amusing others, he or she will be encouraged to look at the lighter side of life. With luck your children might fall into the habit of viewing life with a healthy well developed sense of humor. What better gift could a parent give?...

Funny Business

Personal contract for adding a light touch to my life.

I, (name)_____

promise to

_____
_____
_____.

These changes will be started by (date)

_____. I may need to play with other

people in order to fulfill this contract.

(Names)_____

_____
_____

I cheerfully sign this contract from me to me for me, feeling happy with the knowledge that I am about to be more lighthearted.

Signature_____

Date_____

Chapter Four

Humor and Education

or

Putting Levity in Learning

The auditorium is packed, standing room only, for History of Art 401. Half the college students who have assembled are not even signed up for the course. They have come to hear, watch and experience an extraordinary teacher. Although Ms. Blair is barely 30, her teaching style is already legendary on campus. Using props, costumes and face masks in addition to slides and overheads, she brings fresh insights to works of art, familiar and obscure. Her lectures always draw laughter and applause, and frequently end with a standing ovation.

Twenty-five years later, my friend Marilyn, now in her mid-40s, recalls her most memorable teacher. She can visualize the woman, hear the voice, and recall the titles and content of some of the lectures. "She wasn't a joke-teller," Marilyn recalls. "There was a natural humor in the way she presented herself and the way she presented the subject."

Think back on your favorite teachers in grade school, high school and college — those who really influenced your personal development and excited your interest in learning. If you were to describe those teachers, I'll bet some of the words that would surface are "enthusiastic," "creative" and "funny."

If you are a teacher, a trainer or a member of some related profession, this chapter will show you how to develop and build on these characteristics.

But what if you're not a teacher and no longer a student? Is this information still relevant? Absolutely! Nearly all of us periodically find ourselves in teaching situations:

- ❀ mentoring a junior staff member;
- ❀ showing the new boss how to access the data base;
- ❀ leading a bible study group at church;
- ❀ coaching a neighborhood soccer team;
- ❀ helping your teenager practice parallel parking;
- ❀ showing a toddler how to tie his shoe.

Life is filled with "teachable moments." They don't all happen with your back to the blackboard. Even in the example we set as citizens, workers or parents, we are teachers. And of course, at the other end of the spectrum, we never stop being learners.

Teachers Have Class

Inside or outside of the classroom, you don't need a K-12 teaching certificate to successfully inform, influence and motivate others. If I were writing a classified ad to recruit the ideal teaching candidate, that ad would list these qualifications:

Curiosity. Knowledge of the subject matter is a given; but beyond this base of knowledge, an effective teacher has the desire to keep learning about it. Curiosity keeps us asking questions, researching the subject, exploring new angles. New information enlivens a teaching presentation — gives it a dynamic, up-to-the-minute image. Curiosity reminds us we have much to learn from our workshop participants and students.

Flexibility. A teacher must always be prepared to switch gears. I was scheduled to present a lecture on humor to a University of Michigan psychology class on January 17, 1991 — the day the United States began bombing Iraq. The mood was very somber. "Let's see how we can incorporate humor into a discussion of these world events," I suggested. A funny lecture would have been totally inappropriate, but this put the subject of humor into a different perspective.

One example I recycled from an old gag was a beginning to my theory. I told the story of a four year old boy coming out to the back porch of his house the day after a night of bombing. Holding his mother's hand tightly, he looked up at her and said, "I didn't do it, Mommy!"

This led to a discussion of humor as a stress reliever and opened up a stream of give and take that made the hour fly swiftly by. At the end of class, the students remained and talked for a long while about how they had used humor in stressful situations to attempt to lighten things up.

For the next several classes I was delighted to receive newspaper articles showing how Israeli papers were able to laugh at some of the horror and anguish of the bombings, and other examples.

Sometimes the horror of a situation is so great, it's difficult to open up and talk about it. Humor and a light touch even in times of disaster may help people defuse and de-stress.

Enthusiasm. Put yourself back in high school. Some classes were a

43

blur of toneless lectures and reading assignments. Whatever spark of interest you might have brought to the subject was doused by the listless presenter. Yet other teachers were so enthusiastic they made you care about subjects you never expected to care about. Expertise can be acquired. But excitement about a subject commands other people's attention and sustains their interest.

Sense of humor. You knew this would be on the list! As I've said, it doesn't mean a knack for telling jokes. It can mean the ability to illustrate a point with an appropriate humorous anecdote or spontaneously to play off someone else's comment. A sense of humor can be the ability to think on your feet, keeping a discussion energetic, focused and lively.

Building On Experience

My own background has been as a trainer rather than a teacher. The two are similar except that as a teacher you are usually conveying new information about a previously unknown subject. As a trainer, you are often preparing people to use skills they already have in new ways. Sometimes trainers teach people how to do their jobs better or, in turn, how to teach parts of their job to others. Teaching involves people of all ages, but training almost always involves adults. I have always felt that training is not a punishment...it's a perk!

A classroom of adults is quite different from a classroom of children. Besides being younger and shorter, children are usually free of the preconceived notions and biases that can influence adult learning. "A child's mind is like a clean slate," as one elementary school teacher puts it. "Mixing blue and yellow to make green is a brand new exciting concept."

An adult mind is no blank slate. It's been written on, erased, revised and rewritten with layers upon layers of beliefs and expectations. "Mix blue and yellow? Dark blue or light? How much of each? What happens if you add red? Why are we doing this? How long will it take?"

Adult learners must integrate new ideas with everything they've learned and believed in the past. An effective teacher respects and builds on that experience, recognizing that even though the adults have come to learn, they have a lifetime of wisdom to contribute.

Humor can be a powerful tool to bring forth that experience in positive ways. Suppose you're teaching a workshop for parents on "Surviving the Teenage Years." If you can persuade the participants to reach back into the past and remember their own adolescence — peer pressures, dating disasters and so on — you may be able to stir some humorous common memories. Events that seemed catastrophic at 15 can seem pretty amusing 20 or 30 years later. And the recognition that "some day you'll laugh at this" puts everyone into a positive frame of mind for sharing solutions.

But while experience can be a very good teacher, it can also make us set in our ways. Ever attended a computer workshop? "Technophobia is much more common among adults than children," says Gavin, a software training consultant. "Young children take to a computer terminal like ducks to water. To them it's like a new interesting toy. But many adults freeze at the prospect of all that power and technology."

Humor is useful in these situations as well. Gavin uses exaggeration to break the ice. "The only thing you have to be afraid of is striking two keys simultaneously," he assures the adult learners. "If that happens, you'll wipe out the entire national data base of all of the United States and Canada."

One of the most effective ways to reduce tension is to make a threatening situation seem preposterous.

Education fosters growth, and growth is change. And for most of us, change is a little scary. The status quo, even when it's not entirely satisfying, is more comfortable. Sameness is predictable. Change thrusts you into the unknown.

Humor cushions the landing.

How's This For Openers?

If you are a teacher, a big part of your job occurs before you even begin to share information. Gaining and holding the students' attention, whether they are aged six, 16 or 60 is a challenge in itself. (And if you think it's tough in September, just wait until May!)

It is said that humor ...

❀ gains attention

❀ aids retention

❀ reduces tension

Those three phrases alone sum up the value of humor in education.

Humor as an attention-getter takes many forms. It could be starting the class or workshop with a riddle, a brain-teaser quiz, a joke or a cartoon on an overhead projector. Remove the caption and ask the students, in teams or individually, to fill in the punchline. Wear an amusing tie or a piece of fun jewelry. Play peppy calliope music or a Sousa march as students file into the classroom to set an upbeat mood and start the thought processes flowing. These tactics are not age-specific. They are as effective in grade school as graduate school.

Still, the trends that have led to a merging of entertainment and education began with the younger set. Some writers trace its beginnings to television. Shows like Captain Kangaroo and Sesame Street began a generation ago to use humor in the form of talking animals, puppets, animation and sight gags as teaching devices to teach everything from the alphabet to social skills.

The message: humor in education is FUNdaMENTAL. The fun comes with the mental!

Some critics blame television for changing our expectations about education. They say television has shortened our collective attention span to 13 minutes (between commercials) and caused us to expect information in short, lively snatches.

If this is true, the die is cast. Why shouldn't learning be fun? I think teachers will experience greater success from learning which is enjoyable rather than heavy and serious.

Though primarily known for his animated cartoons, Walt Disney was in the forefront of education. His philosophy was that effective education ... demanded 85 percent entertainment.

Picture an infant shaking a rattle or pulling at the jungle gym. Education begins with the spirit of play. Why not keep the learning process playful and explorative? Why force it to conform to a structure that is formal, structured and serious?

The Sense in Nonsense

I was teaching a full-day workshop for women on Humor In Families. To get things off to a friendly, lively start, we played a game of "human bingo." The objective was to fill a row of squares on a bingo card by finding other workshop participants fitting such descriptions as "has five or more siblings," "likes to sleep late," "oldest daughter," "considers chocolate one of the basic food groups," etc. The exercise got things off to a roaring start because for 10 minutes, the women were all meeting, talking, laughing and mixing with one another. It introduced the day's subject in a playful way, and it created a feeling of commonality among all those present.

Humor benefits teaching and learning in any educational setting from the kindergarten classroom to corporate training headquarters. Whether it takes the form of a "warm-up" exercise as described above, a brainstorming session or any of the tactics lined up at the end of this chapter, humor benefits the educational process.

47

The Benefits of Humor in Education

It creates a positive learning environment. Research shows that students learn better in a relaxed setting where they feel free to "play" around with ideas.

Two third graders are talking. The first one says, "I just found a condom on the veranda." The other little kid asks, "What's a veranda?" This may be a good way for a teacher or parent to begin the topic of sex and sex education with kids.

It introduces energy into an otherwise passive, sedentary situation. Humor, spontaneity and surprise breaks through the students' preoccupied minds and makes them more alert and ready to learn.

Humor builds "commonality" among the students. When people laugh together, they feel they are experiencing a situation in the same way. It is reassuring to be told, "I feel just the same as you." Nothing conveys this feeling of mutual understanding more than laughing together at the same thing at the same time.

Laughter reduces the stress level of the teacher. Speaking in front of groups remains a huge source of anxiety for most people. Hearing and sharing laughter is a great antidote to stress.

It makes the teacher more approachable. People learn best from a person they feel they can relate to, not an austere authority figure.

Humor decreases discipline problems. It helps defuse aggressive behavior. It decreases the pressure on students to be "perfect."

Humor makes it easier to understand and remember new information. Often it is easier to absorb new concepts if we associate them with an amusing story, a cartoon, an anecdote or a silly acronym.

Humor promotes a positive attitude on the part of both teacher and student. A large body of psychological research shows that positive expectations are often a self-fulfilling prophesy and may be powerful predictors of success in learning and other forms of achievement.

Exercise Your Funny Bone

Over the years I have taken numerous exercise classes. I enjoy exercising and find that the instructors who add humor to the routine always get the largest classes and the highest evaluations. Some playful aerobic teachers encourage students to use "the other right leg" or state sweetly after multiple repetitions of movement on both legs "Aren't you glad you don't have three legs?" One class I remember with great fondness was a Yoga lesson with a wonderfully creative teacher. After getting us all into postures we couldn't believe on our shoulders, legs in the air, she announced cheerfully that the class photographer had just entered the room to take our group photograph. She proved my point — it's impossible to be tense while laughing!

Spice Up Your Presentations

Humor in teaching (as elsewhere) should appear to be spontaneous. In reality, it can benefit from carefully laid groundwork. Teachers prepare lesson plans that include lectures, discussion and exams. Shouldn't laughter and play be part of the plan as well?

Think of the following ideas as a spice rack of tips and tactics to season and enhance the flavor of your teaching presentations.

Icebreakers and warm-up exercises. These should get you off to a good start in thinking of ways to mix laughing and learning. The "caption this cartoon" handout or other brain ticklers like the "human bingo" game serve many purposes. They introduce the subject, increase receptivity, and establish a bond between teacher and students. An important caveat: keep these exercises short and within the context of your subject.

Humorous films and audiovisuals. British actor/comedian John Cleese of Monty Python fame has produced some of the most effective training films on the market today. The films poke fun at bad habits to teach subjects like management skills and customer relations. Likewise, a funny overhead transparency may leave a lasting impression. "Humor holds attention and relaxes the audience," Cleese says. "When people remember the joke, they recall the message."

Toys and other Props. A workshop leader uses water from a pitcher, dripping on a sponge, to demonstrate the accumulation of stress. As the water seeps through the sponge and splashes onto the floor, she says, "Sometimes we can't hold in the problems." A science teacher uses a backward-flipping wind-up toy dog to illustrate one of the laws of physics. A trainer uses puzzles, blocks and tongue depressors to reinforce leadership training principles. Magic tricks, lighted earrings, playful jewelry and headgear are integral to my humor presentations — the audience is always waiting to see what I'll do (or don) next!

Reverse student/teacher roles. Ask for a volunteer to teach class occasionally. And you sit in that student's seat. A lot can be learned from this experience!

Simulations. On the third day of a conference on the impact of relocation of older adults, the teacher rearranged the room. Instead of facing the blackboard, the participants were facing the rear window. We (participants) felt disoriented and confused, much as an elderly person would feel after being moved to a new living space. Vaseline smeared on eyeglasses to simulate impaired vision is another way to send this message.

Brainteasers. Flash a puzzle on the overhead projector and ask people to suggest solutions. If you want to promote teamwork in problem solving, put the participants in groups. Game and puzzle books from the library or book stores are full of ideas from which you can adapt or improvise. (See samples at the end of the chapter.)

Brainstorming. The rule is: get all ideas on the table, no matter how wacky or ludicrous. Apply the DOVE system:

Defer judgment;

Offbeat ideas;

Vast number of ideas;

Expand on ideas — let each idea spin off five others.

Brainstorming stimulates creativity and laughter, which are closely related.

Cartoons are a playful yet powerful means of relaying a message. In groups of three to five, assign students to draw cartoons depicting the subject at hand. Encourage stick figures — a Norman Rockwell rendering is not the objective here. Display the cartoons on a board and have a representative from each group describe to the class the issues being addressed. This exercise is fun and serves as an important vehicle for discussing positive and negative attitudes about a topic or situation which might otherwise go unmentioned. Students often report an instant comprehension of the material as a result.

Positive Feedback. Make it easy. Tell the audience: thumbs up if you agree with what I'm saying; thumbs down if you're confused. Ask for mid-semester evaluations in addition to waiting until the course is ended. What am I doing right? What do you want more of?

Take AIM (Acronyms In Moderation). How many can you come up with? ACRONYM = All Creative Representatives Of New York Musicians. APPALLING = Acronym Production Particularly At Lavish Level Is No Good.

Stories and Anecdotes. Young children remember and treasure favorite bedtime stories. I grew up listening to the radio. Inner Sanctum was real and terrifying to me. Stories conjure up visual memories that stick. Facts are static. Stories engage the imagination and later, trigger our memories.

Reversal. Instead of lecturing on the qualities of a good educational experience, have the students brainstorm the characteristics of the worst classroom environment they can imagine. Reversing and exaggerating things at their worst helps us envision them at their best.

Bring back great old word play games such as Tom Swifties. "Someone stole your wheels," said the cop tirelessly. "Your account is up to date," said the banker with interest. "We'll have a rehearsal soon," said the conductor directly. "I am partial to Hemingway," she said earnestly. "Here's your sunburn lotion," said Lola soothingly. "You failed the exam," the teacher said testily.

Humor Homeplay. For one week reverse the way you have your toilet paper on the roller. If you are an "over the roll" person, position it against the wall. And if you are an "against the wall" type, over it goes! This assignment will not only remind you to look at things from different angles and different perspectives, it also prevents hardening of the attitudes! Reversing things — changing the route to work, sitting in a different chair at home and even reading the newspaper beginning with a different section — is another way to remind yourself to change attitudes from force of habit to farce of habit.

Put Humor to the Test. Insert a humorous question, multiple choice selection or the names of some storybook or cartoon characters in your next multiple choice quiz. Mention the firm of Flopsy, Mopsy and Cottontail in the next legal issues exam. Slipping in something unexpected raises the students' attention level and may even raise their test scores!

I encourage you to experiment with these humor ingredients, using them liberally in your workshop presentations or lesson plans. But remember, humor is the spice, not the dish itself. Humor in teaching, like cinnamon or bay leaf in a recipe, must be used in proportion to the overall content. Too much laughter can get in the way of substance. It's a matter of balance.

The key rule is: make the humor relevant to the context of the subject. Then it becomes part of a lesson instead of a diversion from it.

Laughter can maximize learning.

In Other Words...

It has long been known that...

I haven't bothered to look up the original source.

Of great theoretical and practical importance...

I find it interesting.

It is suggested that...it is believed... It may be that...

I think so.

It is generally believed...

Two other guys think so, too.

It is obvious...

I think that's the way it should be, but I can't explain it.

While it has not been possible to provide a definitive answer to the question...

The experiment didn't work out, but I figured I could get a publication out of it.

Typical results are shown...

The results of all the others was pure gibberish.

Results are applicable within an order of magnitude...

The results are wrong.

It is clear that much additional work will be required before a complete understanding is...

I don't understand this.

Unfortunately, a viable quantitative theory to account for the results has yet to be formulated...

Nobody else understands it either.

53

Chapter Five

Humor in the Workplace

or

Laughter: The Best Job Perk

Employers are forever searching for a formula that will increase productivity, reduce tension and boost morale.

The formula is here and it's deceptively simple:

Mix business with pleasure.

Forget "the daily grind," the salt mines, the countdown to retirement. You can do away with these negative images. Some people would even trade the slogan, "TGIF" for "Thank God It's Monday."

Having fun at work is no longer considered a contradiction. Research bears out what smart managers know instinctively: humor enhances work performance. It's right up there with fax machines and personal computers.

Workplace humor can take many forms, slight to significant:

❀ Describing a funny incident at the beginning of a tense staff meeting

❀ Putting a whimsical sign on your desk

❀ Publishing a humorous April Fool's Day spoof of the in-house newsletter

❀ Posting a cartoon on the office bulletin board

❀ Seeking out — and pointing out — positive trends in a bad budget year

"The most important asset in business is a sense of humor, an ability to laugh at yourself or the situation," states Mark McCormick, author of *What They Don't Teach You in Harvard Business School*.

Take, for example, Chrysler Chairman Lee Iacoca. He's no knee-slapping comedian, but he is comfortable and at ease exchanging jokes with reporters at a press conference or with shareholders at the annual meeting. His humor puts others at ease and enhances his image as a leader who is affable and in control. It deflects criticism and rivets the audience's attention to what he has come to say.

What works for the chairman of the board works up and down the corporate ladder. An even temperament and a positive outlook bond you with your colleagues and your competitors, your supervisors and subordinates.

The message here is not to make fun of work, but to **have fun at work.**

Are You Having Fun Yet?

Try this non-scientific but potentially revealing True/False quiz:

    T   F

1. __ __ I approach my job with high expectations, anticipation and enthusiasm.
2. __ __ The people I work with would say I have a good sense of humor.
3. __ __ I can handle a little kidding. People don't hesitate to tease me for fear I'll take it the wrong way.
4. __ __ I can also laugh at myself. I treat my mistakes as a valuable learning experience.
5. __ __ At office parties, I often give light-hearted gag gifts and funny cards.
6. __ __ I enjoy non-competitive games and contests and often help plan or conduct them.
7. __ __ I always seek out humorous Post-It notes, signs, posters and other whimsical office decor.
8. __ __ I enjoy the people I work with. I can find good qualities in almost everybody.
9. __ __ I continually look for new creative ways to do routine or repetitive tasks.
10. __ __ I purposely seek out the funny, ironic side of life and share it with others.
11. __ __ I smile and laugh a lot at work, even during periods of stress.
12. __ __ My work is so rewarding, I would (almost) do it for free!

This is a self-scoring quiz. Give yourself 5 points for each T response, 0 for F. The higher your score, the higher your worktime Humor Quotient.

Only you can decide what ratio of true vs. false — fun vs. drudgery — is acceptable for you.

Funny Business

"What's so funny about work?

"If your answer is 'plenty!' you could be one of the most productive and creative workers in your company," writes Lona O'Connor, in her syndicated column, "Working."

"Humor can serve many important functions, " O'Connor explains.

It reduces anger, tension and boredom which wear down a worker's efficiency.

It can break up fights before they start to boil over.

It makes people feel friendlier toward each other.

It helps maintain the broad perspective, which can relieve the constant worrier.

It starts ideas rolling."

O'Connor is not just stating a hunch; she's backed up by a growing body of research on humor and work performance. One small but often-cited study was conducted in the mid-80s by David J. Abramis, an organizational psychologist at California State University at Long Beach.

Abramis surveyed workers in a variety of white collar professions asking them about fun at work, which he defined as "enjoyment, pleasure and amusement derived from working."

"It appears that in the absence of fun, people in the workplace are more anxious, depressed, perform tasks more poorly and don't get along as well with others," he reports.

"In contrast, employees who enjoy some level of fun on the job worked longer hours and got more accomplished. They were less likely to be late, absent or bored, and they remained longer with the company."

This study hit the wire services and has been enthusiastically cited in media across the country. It offers further evidence that people consider humor important.

So does Adia, a personnel placement service organization with head-quarters in Menlo Park, California. It surveyed 1,160 human resources profes-sionals about what humorous practices their companies use to boost morale and relieve job stress. The results:

    ❀   Seventy-seven percent tell a joke to break the ice at a staff meeting;

    ❀   Seventy-five percent encourage employees to display humorous cartoons or comic strips;

    ❀   Fifty-two percent use humor to lighten deadline pressure;

    ❀   Thirty-nine percent promote "laugh breaks" among their employees;

    ❀   Fifty percent think hiring a "humor consultant" to train employees to lighten up is a viable idea.

The evidence is mounting: a playful attitude pays big dividends in mediating stress, building rapport and stimulating creativity.

There is also a strong link between entrepreneurial talent and the word FUN. Most successful, inventive entrepreneurs characterize their work as fun. Their enjoyment of the process leads them to be more creative, to test new ideas and to be more productive.

Time flies and creativity soars when you're having fun.

The Creativity Connection

This item, creativity, is powerfully important. Great ideas often spring from fun and nonsense. Like a firecracker lights up the Fourth of July sky, laughter unlocks the slumbering circuits of the brain.

When we imagine a lively, creative work setting, one of the first fields that comes to mind is advertising. Advertising agencies conjure up an image of Peter Max neckties and basketball hoops over wastebaskets. Surely no one thought up 1989's award-winning Eveready bunny commercials while seated in a somber, sedate boardroom.

Carmichael-Lynch, an ad agency in Minneapolis, seems to run on fun. It holds an annual Pet Day when employees are encouraged to bring pets to the office to show off stupid pet tricks. On St. Patrick's Day, they hold a talent contest, "the O'Gong Show," complete with a six-foot diameter gong. Co-owner Lee Lynch supports this foolishness. His desk bears the sign: "Remember, advertising is not open-heart surgery."

"This is such an intense business," Lynch explained in a newspaper interview. "With highs very high and lows very low, we need to have a way to channel that emotion in a constructive way."

Humor can link creativity with problem-solving in all kinds of work settings.

Psychologist Alice M. Isen demonstrated this principle with research subjects at the University of Maryland in Baltimore. Several groups of people were each given a candle, matches and a box of tacks. Their task was to attach the candle to a corkboard in such a way that it would not drip wax on the floor when it was lighted.

The solution was to empty that tacks out of the box so that it could be attached to the board as a candle holder. Groups who had seen a funny film just before taking this test solved the problem *three times faster* than those who watched an educational film about mathematics, Isen reported.

"When people are in a good mood, they tend to combine their ideas in new ways," the study concluded. "Humor helps us react more broadly and creatively to an intellectual challenge."

Many of us remember sitting in meetings where silly ideas were tossed about like paper airplanes. Occasionally, someone would take hold of one of those ideas, give it a new spin, and turn it into something brilliant.

The best ideas rarely come in tidy little boxes. They come bouncing off the wall. "Off the wall" can mean anyplace that's unpredictable and unexpected. Creativity happens when you are able to shift your attention from "why it won't work," to "what's good about it?"

Laughter keeps us loose and mentally fit. Thinking positively, we're able to generate ideas and ultimately to come up with better solutions.

The Corporate Culture

In a fast-paced world that promotes power breakfasts, "networking" in the guise of socializing, rituals and rules, there's a notable absence of playfulness in many work environments.

We no longer cheer ourselves by buying a frivolous hat; we "dress for success." Many of us turn hobbies and sports into goal-oriented tasks to excel in, not activities to be enjoyed. For many grownups, the closest experience to "playing" is going to the gym for a workout.

Notice the word is *workout*.

Part of this is a function of the "corporate culture." Your workplace has an emotional environment whether you work for a corporation like General Motors or for a community college or a retail shop or fast food chain.

Some organizations actively promote and institutionalize merriment. The Carmichael-Lynch agency is one example. Ben and Jerry's Homemade Ice Cream plant in Waterbury, Vermont is another. They have a standing committee called the Joy Gang. This group takes a hands-on approach to fun, for example, hiring a massage therapist to give every worker a 15-minute massage.

Other companies create more traditional opportunities for fun: time out for office birthday celebrations or date-of-hire anniversary parties, company-sponsored softball leagues or interdepartmental contests and special events. If your workplace doesn't have a Cheers Committee, maybe you're just the person to start one.

Even more effortless: institute a humor bulletin board near the copy machine or coffee lounge. Cover it with amusing cartoons, clips and comic strips, funny postcards, newspaper articles, buttons, gags, whatever tickles your funny bone.

It shouldn't contain information on serious matters like the union notices and fire drill instructions. There's plenty of room for that on the official bulletin board.

Make it a *rotating* responsibility. Finding out what amuses someone you don't know very well — or don't like very much — could help you get to know that person in a different way.

Pulling Your Own Strings

Ultimately the responsibility for finding more humor in our work life rests with us. It doesn't happen by accident. Each of us, from the boss to the newest employee, plays a role in creating a positive work climate.

"A sense of humor is one of the basic traits that distinguishes people from animals. The problem is that many business people believe that they must appear absolutely serious at all times," says Malcolm Kushner, author of *The Light Touch*. "And it's actually counterproductive to conducting business effectively."

It has nothing to do with telling one-liners or wearing a clown suit. As Lona O'Connor writes, "Don't trade in your sensible suit for an orange wig and floppy shoes. As any good joke-teller knows, timing is everything. Use humor only when it can have a good effect. Being funny all the time will only brand you the office yo-yo."

It goes without saying that humor should never be at anyone else's expense. Jokes that belittle a co-worker or a client could create enemies and quickly land you on unemployment compensation.

Making jokes at your own expense is another story. Self-deprecating humor, used sparingly, can win people over, especially if you are the newly-hired supervisor or an outside consultant meeting with resistance from the office team.

Not only is humor good in sales and marketing, it can help deal with unpleasant sales attempts. Most people seem to be irritated and angry with telephone solicitations. Charlotte, a nurse, handles phone solicitors in a way that amuses her. After being asked by a strange voice on the phone the usual, "And how are you this evening, Mrs. Hanson?" she quickly starts to respond with a list of disgusting ailments. One time she might say, "Oh I'm feeling terrible, I just vomited some green fluid and I have diarrhea, and a pounding headache and my left arm is swollen," and on and on. It may not be nice, but it is her way of smiling about this intrusion instead of becoming annoyed.

Malcolm Kushner uses self-effacing humor to his advantage when warming up a new audience. He often opens by mentioning that he used to be a practicing attorney. "Whether or not you think the world needs a humor consultant, I'm sure you'll agree that we can use one less lawyer," he says. The audience laughs in agreement. and Kushner has built instant rapport with the participants.

Poking fun at ourselves humanizes us. While some people — especially managers — fear a loss of authority, it actually has the opposite effect. It projects confidence and reduces the artificial barriers that get in the way of doing our best work.

Take your work seriously but yourself lightly!

Twelve Ways to Lighten Up

Fun at work falls into two distinct categories, according to Abramis' study:

- ❀ company-sponsored activities such as the aforementioned birth-day celebrations and sports teams, and
- ❀ joy in the work itself.

The happiest people found pleasure in the daily process of designing, selling, marketing or managing their assigned tasks. Social contact with friends and co-workers was a large part of their job satisfaction, as were good relationships with their supervisors and subordinates.

Here, in review, are a dozen ways to lighten up your work load:

1. Seek out cartoons to pass around, post or publish.
2. Display a whimsical sign, toy or stuffed animal in your work space.
3. Designate a central bulletin board for humor, and rotate the responsibility for updating it.
4. Hold a baby photo contest.
5. Start a humor file.
6. Add a humorous quote, cartoon or joke to the office newsletter.
7. Have a caption-writing contest for a cartoon related to an issue at work.
8. Give a nickname to the computer, the copier, the FAX machine.
9. Team up for an afterwork softball game or bowling league.
10. Hold a Rube Goldberg brainstorming session to devise the silliest way to accomplish a task.
11. Celebrate birthdays and anniversaries of date-of-hire.
12. Thank someone with a balloon bouquet.

13. Serve "happy" food such as ice cream cones, popcorn or lolli-pops at staff meetings.

Intrinsic job satisfaction has to come from within. But we can create more opportunities for it to happen. And, since many of us spend close to half our waking hours at work, job satisfaction is a big part of life satisfaction.

Chapter Six

Celebrations

My cousin Ruth had been planning her daughter's wedding since the child's birth. Finally the day arrived, and it was destined to be the most memorable event in the history of Dayton, Ohio. Months of preparation had gone into ensuring that everything would be perfect.

The flowers were ordered, the orchestra hired, and to make the event even more special, the bride's family reserved a newly-opened posh hotel for the wedding reception. It was to be the first event ever held in the hotel's beautiful top floor banquet hall.

The great evening arrived. The guests were all dressed in elegant attire — the women in long formal gowns, the men in dinner jackets. After a lovely ceremony and sit-down dinner came the grand finale. The lights dimmed, the orchestra played a chord, the drums rolled, and out from the kitchen marched a parade of waiters, each bearing a large platter of flaming cherries jubilee.

Around and around the banquet hall they marched to the music, holding the trays of flaming cherries like torches high above their heads...

...setting off the restaurant's newly-installed automatic sprinkler system.

Like a fine but steady spring rain the water fell, dousing the cherries and drenching the wedding guests. The stunned silence was finally broken by a giggle. It bubbled and grew into gales of laughter.

As a memorable event, my cousin's daughter's wedding had surpassed all expectations!

Cymbals and Fireworks

If we were to draw a timeline of life events, it is often the celebrations that stand out in our memories: the births and birthdays; weddings (even ones less eventful than the one just described); anniversaries, graduations and retirement parties; holidays, vacations and reunions.

On the landscape of life, celebrations are like wildflowers dotting a rolling green meadow, or stars across the canvas of dark evening sky.

Routine tasks and events blur in our memories, but the celebrations remain vivid, possibly because we fortify them with anticipation and high hopes. Afterwards we enjoy looking back on them, spinning them over and over like favorite records on the turntable of our minds.

Sometimes celebrations don't quite live up to our expectations, but often they exceed anything we could have imagined.

Like my cousin's daughter's wedding, celebrations contain many of the characteristics we've learned to associate with humor: exaggeration, reversal, surprise.

Exaggeration: the fancy food, decorated setting or our own party attire.

Reversal: an ordinary day is turned into something special and extraordinary.

Surprise: lurks in the midst of celebrations. At a child's birthday party, for example, the surprises include games, entertainment, gifts and party favors.

Celebrations mean:

❀ laughter	❀ surprises
❀ friendship	❀ spontaneity
❀ games	❀ silliness
❀ music	❀ dressing up
❀ color	❀ decorations
❀ food	❀ playfulness
❀ fun	❀ close feelings
❀ souvenirs	❀ memories

You can extend this list as far as your imagination.

The message of this chapter is: if you want to put more humor and fun in your life, create more celebrations.

Cause for Celebration

The first rule of journalism consists of writing a complete opening paragraph. It must answer "the 5 W's" — <u>W</u>ho, <u>W</u>hat, <u>W</u>hen, <u>W</u>here and <u>W</u>hy.

Planning a party or celebration focuses on these same elements.

Who

People are clearly the most important element in any gathering, planned or spontaneous. You as the organizer may supply the theme, setting and props. The participants provide the warmth, laughter and good feelings.

` You could invite anyone you know and like as well as anyone you'd like to know better. The guests needn't know each other; celebrations are a happy excuse to enlarge your circle of friends.

` You might even include people you *don't* know, as when you're hosting a baby shower and invite friends of the mother-to-be whom you've never met.

` You might choose people with something in common. We once held a Brooklyn Party, inviting our Ann Arbor friends who'd grown up in that city. We played childhood games like stick ball and ringalevio and served Nathan's hot dogs and charlotte russe.

When

Don't be locked into thinking that celebrations should only take place on Saturday nights. Nor do they need to be keyed to a special occasion like New Year's Eve or a 50th birthday. When celebrations occur at unexpected times for offbeat reasons, the element of surprise kicks in:

- ❀ It's never too late!!! Growing up in New York City, few of us owned cars. In 1947, my date and I took the subway to my high school prom. For my 60th birthday, my children gave me a three hour limousine ride around town!
- ❀ Celebrate the seasons: not just the traditional holidays but Washington's Birthday, Groundhog Day, the first snowfall, the spring thaw.
- ❀ Celebrate achieving a minor milestone: losing 10 pounds, coming home from the hospital, passing inspection, finishing final exams,

cleaning the attic.

❀ Order a deli tray for the office staff to celebrate the end of a record sales quarter.

❀ Invite the neighbors over to view and sniff the dramatic blossom on your night-blooming cereus plant.

❀ One energetic hostess we know uses time to her advantage by holding back-to-back parties. She has one group of friends over for dinner and another group for brunch the next morning. Breads, fruit trays and floral arrangements do double duty. She insists that having two smaller gatherings instead of one large one gives her more time at each to enjoy her guests.

Where

Many people don't get past the "who" and "when" of a celebration because they get blocked by the "where." The place, (usually their home, condo or apartment) is never quite "ready" to receive visitors. An important ground rule of mounting a party or celebration is this: don't wait until the space is perfect. Don't even try to define what "perfect" should be.

When Jane and Ted bought their first home they promised their friends they'd have a housewarming party "after we replace the carpeting." But once the plush new carpeting was installed — you guessed it — it magnified the shabbiness of the wallpaper. The housewarming was put off indefinitely.

Alice and Keith, another pair of new homeowners, had a better idea: they held a "before" party so their friends could see "where we're coming from" before they launched into the redecorating process. (And they didn't have to worry about wine being spilled on the carpet!)

Use these unexpected ways to modify the party environment:

❀ Magnify the flaws. A few days before we had planned an after-the-game football party, our upstairs bath pipes burst causing extensive water damage to the ceiling over our entrance way. Large pieces of plaster fell away, exposing the tangle of pipes and plumbing guts. Instead of canceling the party or trying to camouflage the damage, we hung crepe paper streamers and balloons from the tattered ceiling. (This again illustrates the classic qualities of celebration...exaggeration, reversal, surprise and humor!)

❀ Move the party elsewhere. Four of my women friends celebrated a birthday by having a slumber party at a motel. We swam in the pool, piled into the jacuzzi and stayed up late eating junk food and pizza. Around midnight we decorated the birthday cake with sparklers.

❀ Take your celebration to the guests. When their frail grandparents could not attend their wedding, a thoughtful bride and groom dressed up the next day in their wedding clothes and visited the grandparents at the nursing home. A photographer came along and took pictures.

Never let the limitations of place and space stop you from being festive. You don't have to wax the driveway or float gardenias in the toilet bowl to set the stage for a gathering of friends.

My premise is, it's the people who are important, not the premises.

What and Why

Reasons to celebrate are infinite, and sometimes the best reason is no reason at all.

Celebrations don't require a momentous event. Sometimes they can be mounted around an inventive theme.

A Detroit couple, both artists/writers, host a large outdoor party each summer. One year, several of the guests arrived dressed all in white, and everyone commented how cool, elegant and "F. Scott Fitzgerald-ish" they appeared, and the White Party was born. Now guests for the annual event are requested to wear white. Some come in ethnic, gauzy, flowing robes; others in tennis togs or period costumes such as a beaded 20's dress. Antique white gloves and parasols appear annually, as do hats of all descriptions. The food adds another dimension to the theme: guests are assigned a potluck dish by course and color — a red appetizer, purple vegetable, blue dessert, etc. It is all colorfully laid out before serving, creating, in combination with the guests, a piece of live art.

Baby showers can be a source of silly or even serious advice. Invite guests to write any piece of advice they would give to both parents of the newborn AND the child of the parents. Collect these in an album for a source of instant memories and smiles.

Here are some more examples of no-special-occasion celebrations:

❀ Instead of adding a bonus to its employees' end-of-the-year paychecks, one firm rented a bus, closed early and took the entire staff to a shopping mall. Each person was given two $100 bills and two hours of release time with instructions to spend the money on themselves. This gesture of surprise and reversal gave a big boost to employee morale.

❀ When my children were growing up, we would celebrate earning an A+ on an essay or test. The star pupil would get to choose the dinner menu and would be served on a china plate with good silver and a linen napkin.

❀ After stripping off the old kitchen wallpaper we learned there was a delay before the new paper would arrive. The family decided to hold an art/graffiti contest. We gave everyone paint and brushes and a large portion of wall to decorate as they saw fit. We enjoyed our artwork for several weeks until the new wallpaper arrived. To this day, each family member can describe the artwork under his or her section of the wall.

❀ Celebrations can be a reward for any accomplishment. Celebrate painting the living room by going out to a movie. Celebrate shoveling the driveway by having a snowball fight! (Or, by cozying up indoors with a mug of hot cocoa. Or both!)

❀ Kathy, a 40-year-old teacher, celebrates her wedding anniversary every year by donning her formal fancy wedding dress and cooking breakfast for her family as a bride. The dress is spattered with pancake grease and coffee stains but has had more use and gained more value than many a cellophane wrapped heirloom.

❀ Some people send their bridal party a card on the anniversary of *their* wedding. This serves as a regular opportunity to keep in touch with friends who may have moved away.

❀ Cheryl, a graduate student, has created a ritual among her friends. She holds a PMS Party, inviting her friends to attend with stringy hair, decorating her apartment with Tampax and serving a wide selection of chocolate bars. Laugh — and the world laughs with you!

❀ After an unhappy marriage of 27 years, a newly divorced woman felt the need to commemorate this new phase of life. She decided to give herself a "Divorce Party." She invited old friends, asking them to invite someone she didn't know to her party in order to add new people new lifestyle. She decorated her home with bunches of snapdragons and served deviled eggs and devil's food cake and felt exorcised from her ex-husband. A lively time was had by all, and the woman experienced a much-needed sense of closure.

The previous examples sum up all the best reasons to celebrate, including *who* should be involved (anyone we care about, starting with ourselves); *where* (any gathering place is sufficient); *what*, (any occasion), *why* (any reason) and *when*, (when the mood strikes, and as often as possible).

Let the Festivities Begin

I speak to many people who are involved in caregiving situations and support groups. A woman in the audience once asked me wistfully, "What support group do you join if you like joy and fun?"

Thinking over my circle of family and friends, I realized that they constitute just such a support system. I know I can depend on them in a time of crisis. But if I need someone to share in a moment of joy and fun, they are equally ready to rise to the occasion!

So many hosts try to plan parties to perfection, yet some of the most memorable parties are far from perfect. Humor permits us to laugh at our imperfections and mistakes. It humanizes us.

Imperfect sets the theme for several playful parties that are favorites among my friends:

❀ "The Mother of the Bride Dress Party." Finally, a second chance to show off the flowing peach chiffon with the dyed-to-match satin shoes. It was never quite right for the supermarket. Alice, a 58-year-old writer, hosted a Mother of the Bride/Groom Dress Party at her home. The hit of the evening was the hostess wearing her 12-year-old mother-of-the-bride dress proudly. The fact that she had gained almost 20 pounds since her daughter's wedding did not deter her. She creatively left the back unzipped and used colorful shoelaces to keep the dress in place. Everyone had a wonderful time!

73

- ❀ "The Bridesmaid Dress Party," (adapted by my daughter from the theme above). Remember how the bride assured you you'd wear it — with its Little Bo Peep bow in the back — "again and again?" This event proved her right!
- ❀ Al, a soon to be groom, and a wine enthusiast, is taking an active role in the planning of his wedding and reception. He is selecting a fine dinner wine and plans on purchasing 50 extra bottles to be stored away. His plan is to open a bottle on each anniversary and talk about the fine times of the past year at an anniversary dinner.
- ❀ "The Mistake Party." A third variation on the costume theme. Search your closet: this outfit probably still has the fifth mark-down tag on it.
- ❀ "The Leftover Party." A great chance to free up some freezer space.

One hostess holds an annual "Miss America Party," on the same night as the pageant. The guests, all women, are asked to wear a bathing suit or evening gown and to show off their talent. Upon arrival, each of us receives a sash upon which to create our name. I have been Miss Understand, Miss Demeanor and Miss Cellaneous at past parties. The refreshments are "All-American" like American cheese, apple pie, hot dogs and lemonade. We follow the format of the pageant in a most irreverent way while the television in the background relays the events from Atlantic City. This eagerly-anticipated gathering guarantees against taking oneself too seriously!

The Advantage of Guestwork

All of the above ideas emphasize that one key to a successful celebration is involvement. The guests are not passive recipients, but partici-pants in the production.

I love to give dinner parties, but I hate to be stuck alone in the kitchen while the guests are enjoying drinks in the living room. Why should they have all the fun? For our Chinese New Year dinner party, each guest comes ready to prepare a chosen dish. We supply an apron and a cleaver. Each person or couple gets their turn at the wok preparing an entree. My husband and I provide drinks, hors d'oeuvres and a main dish. The cooks do their magic in turn, presenting their dish with fanfare. And the dishes are served one at a time. We can really savor each. Everyone gets into the act of cooking, eating and having fun.

Even an event as traditional as a wedding needn't be predictable or overly solemn. One creative mother of the groom planned a rehearsal dinner that generated many new acquaintances. All of the guests received name tags, upon which we were to write a positive adjective with the same letter as our first name. I therefore sported the tag "Lively Lila" that evening. Her first "icebreaker" was a large board with photographs of the bride and groom, their siblings and others in the wedding party along with their baby pictures. By matching the pictures correctly we each won a prize. Aware that many family friends from both sides had not met, the hostess also devised a game of "Wedding Bingo." Each of us had a sheet of paper with 25 squares to fill out: find a person who has your same birthday month, someone who loves chocolate, someone born in a different state, and so on. In the process of filling our Bingo squares, we each got to know a large cross section of our fellow guests and things we had in common. The activities of this rehearsal party made the wedding reception seem like a gathering of old friends.

My neighbor is part of a large family that gets together rarely, so he hosts a family reunion every Fourth of July weekend. Their tradition is to provide a birthday cupcake for each member of the clan. After blowing out the single candle, each honoree must tell the funniest thing that happened to him or her during the past year.

Most memorable experiences consist of three parts:
- ❀ Anticipation
- ❀ Participation
- ❀ Recapitulation

A joyful occasion combines all three, and frequently becomes a treasured memory to play back again and again.

Our large family home on Martin Place held many such memories.

When the time came to move after 28 years, my husband and I and our children couldn't help but feel mixed emotions about leaving this place that had been "part of the family." So we held a "house cooling" party with a traditional Thanksgiving dinner — in March! — and shared memories around the table. We each described one of our happiest moments and laughed over the crises. This event gave us a much-needed sense of closure and helped us deal with our mixed emotions — while emphasizing the happy ones.

Celebrate Life

We usually think of celebrations as social gatherings like dinners, parties and dinner parties. But celebrations can be any little note of cheer and triumph —

* a sign in the front yard that announces "It's a Girl!"
* a congratulatory phone call.
* a rose on your secretary's desk.
* a greeting card that says "I'm glad we're friends."
* a banner across the doorway that says "Welcome home!"

Celebrations represent another form of caring and communication. Even a family newsletter becomes a celebration of life:

When her husband Jack underwent surgery and chemotherapy for cancer, his wife Ellen reassured concerned family and friends with a series of newsletters chronicling his recovery. In place of the ominous words, "Jack underwent surgery," she wrote: "Jack entertained Drs. Miller, Newton and a chorus of nurses and technicians for seven hours, exposing his innermost secrets to the startled crew."

Duly reporting the surgery and its potential complications, she inserted footnotes such as:

"Jack doomed by amorous wife to strenuous exercise around the house." and

"Ellen now owes 30¢ for gin rummy losses, not covered by health plan."

Ellen's newsletter again illustrates the power of humor to cast perspective on a serious subject. She didn't gloss over or trivialize her husband's condition as she briskly described the "surgical redesign of lower abdomen: tumor removed, rectum shut off and more convenient aperture designed into wall of tum." But she emphasized not the illness but the feisty recovery of his "astonishing body."

Living is as much an attitude as it is a process. It often comes down to the old question: is our glass half empty or half full?

My daughter Sue owns a calendar/journal diary with the days listed, but not the year. Whenever she has a particularly good or happy time she writes it down in the book. Her focus is on the joyful, happy feelings. Her intention is to keep this journal and to have "celebrated" a whole year's worth of good days!

Sylvia, a mother and mother-in-law of two newly divorced young adult children, hated to part with the lovely wedding photos on her family picture wall. She handled the situation by pasting the "slash/circle" No Smoking type sign over the "Out-lawed" person.

Life is too full of novelty and hope for us to remain solemn too long.

Happy Endings

When you were a child, did you ever play Let's Pretend? In your imagination you became a princess, a pirate or a cowboy, acting out the script as it evolved in your mind.

Most of us grownups have forgotten how to play. Along with our discarded toys we too often put aside laughter and spontaneity as we enter the sobering world of adulthood. We have become spectators instead of participants, gathering our entertainment from movies, television and sports events.

Little kids have playgroups and playmates. Why not big kids as well?

Adults need to play Let's Pretend for the same reasons children do. It helps us make order of the chaos of everyday living. Humor and playfulness are a channel to our deepest sources of creativity.

We can recapture the spirit of play by engaging our imagination in ordinary, routine tasks. For example:

Barbara Mackoff, author of *Leaving the Office Behind* recommends celebrating the end of the work day with a "closing ceremony." It went something like this:

1. Turn off the computer, the coffee maker and the copying machine.
2. Turn on the telephone answering machine.
3. Tuck away today's work into the appropriate file folders. Tidy up your desk.
4. Turn off the lights and lock the doors.
5. On your way home, roll the credits of your day, just as they would appear at the end of a movie.

When you "roll the credits of your day," you could add the line, "any similarity to persons living or dead is purely coincidental."

And if it was an especially good day, put your name in lights. See yourself accepting the Academy Award or the Nobel Prize for the day's achievements. Graciously acknowledge the audience's enthusiastic applause.

Perhaps we should adapt this idea to the closing of any day. Look in on the children, look after the pets, lock the doors, turn out the lights, shut your eyes, and let those credits roll.

Someone once described life thusly — "You're born — you go on a few diets — and you die." Let's add a bit more fun to this description!

Make every day a celebration of living!

Chapter Seven

Humor and Expression

or

Smiles, Laughter and Tears

If I asked you what humor sounds like, you would probably imagine the sound of laughter. If I asked you what humor looks like, you'd picture a smile.

Smiles are the outward manifestation of everything we associate with good humor — friendliness, happiness, warmth, a positive outlook. They are a universal language, spanning every culture. Smiles, in fact, allow us to communicate without words. They encourage, agree, soothe, flirt and reward. And the list goes on.

One of the smile's chief functions is "feedback." That may sound like psychological jargon, but its simply means the information we get from someone's reaction to what we say or do. It's part of the communication process. Positive feedback brings positive results:

- ✿ Salespeople who smile have more satisfied customers.
- ✿ Managers who smile have more loyal, productive employees.
- ✿ Performers who smile get louder applause.
- ✿ Parents who smile raise more confident children.

Smiles make us look attractive, but even more important, they make us look friendly and responsive. Go to a cocktail party and watch who's getting the most attention. People who smile are perceived as well-liked and approachable. We are naturally attracted to people who smile.

A frown gives the opposite kind of feedback. It may turn people away. A frown sends a message of disapproval. Instead of motivating us to progress, it sends us back to square one.

A frown tells us we've done something wrong but seldom tells us what we should do instead. There's more information in a smile. It says "Right on! You're on the right track! Keep up the good work!" Smiles increase our security and sense of accomplishment. That encouragement opens us up to new experiences. A smile exhilarates us.

Origin of the Species

Why do people smile? Surprisingly, scientists are still uncertain what causes this most basic facial expression. Some theorists noted that chimpan-

zees and other apes bare their teeth in a semi-threatening grin
aggression. Similarly, many humans will smile to prevent an argum

The British naturalist Charles Darwin, known best for his theory of
evolution, noted that the sweet receptors are located at the tip of the tongue.
To maximize the sweet taste of anything we eat, we push the tongue forward.
This movement causes us to open our mouths in a kind of a smile. According to
this logic, sweetness equals smiling.

Darwin also conducted research on the universality of emotional
expressions. He wrote letters to people in the military, churches and government in the far reaches of the British Empire, asking them to describe how
people in those areas expressed grief, fear, joy and other emotions. Now that
we can access other parts of the world with the flick of a television knob, we
know that people in all cultures express pleasure by smiling.

Yet different cultures clearly have different rules. The British are far
more reserved in expressing emotions than, say, the Italians. And for that
matter, people in Boston tend to be more reserved than people in New
Orleans.

Laughter is so important in some cultures, there are even special
ceremonies recognizing this rite of passage. In traditional Navajo Indian
culture, there is a special "First Laugh Ceremony." A baby is constantly
watched over until the child laughs for the first time. This moment marks the
child's birth as a social being. A large lively celebration in honor of this
important happening is shared and enjoyed by family and friends.

Still, all people in all cultures have one thing in common; we each have
a face. This magnificent device uses 80 different muscles to communicate
countless messages ranging from delight to deceit. Learning to "read" other
people's faces gives us information about ourselves and our world. Besides
speaking, it's our major source of social interaction. This communication is at
the core of the human experience.

Say Cheese

It's human nature to seek positive feedback. We can't see ourselves
behave, so we watch one another's faces for approval. We act as mirrors for

one another.

This raises an obvious question: if someone else's smile can make us happy, can smiling produce the same effect in ourselves?

Do we smile because we're happy, or are we happy because we smile? A growing body of research suggests both may be true.

William James stirred the debate nearly a century ago. The psychologist and brother of novelist Henry James took the radical viewpoint that facial expressions caused emotions instead of the other way around. He stated:

"...The more rational statement is that we feel sorry because we cry, angry because we strike, afraid because we tremble, and not that we cry, strike, tremble because we are sorry, angry or fearful, as the case may be."

No one took James too seriously at the time, but researchers at the University of California at San Francisco and the University of Michigan now agree he may have been on to something.

University of California's Paul Ekman has been studying facial expressions for over three decades. With his colleague Wallace Friesin, Eckman developed the Facial Action Coding System in 1978 and has catalogued 50 different kinds of smiles.

He has also determined that facial expressions not only reveal emotions, they can create them as well. Try smiling right now. Did you feel your spirits lift? According to Eckman, manipulating the muscles and the blood vessels of the face may bring about chemical changes in the brain which make us feel happier or sadder.

Robert Zajonc, a psychologist at the University of Michigan and director of the Institute for Social Research, agrees. In his view, the act of smiling and controlled breathing allows more air to flow through the nasal passage, cooling the blood that flows to the brain.

A smile tightens and relaxes various cheek muscles, as when you say "cheese." The cooler blood flow makes you feel better. Frowning or scowling, it turns out, has the opposite effect.

Zajonc says this theory may suggest why thumb sucking is so satisfying to babies. It forces them to breathe through the nose. The brain cooling effect may also release endorphins, the pain-killing chemicals which are also associated with laughter.

This research could also explain why adults get pleasure from gum chewing or pipe smoking, Zajonc says, and why yoga and Lamaze have such a soothing, relaxing effect. All of these increase air flow through the nasal cavity, cooling the brain and causing feelings of mild euphoria.

The findings are still preliminary, the scientists say. Meanwhile, we can experiment on our own by smiling as often as possible. Remember:

A smile increases your face value.

A smile is to a human as a tail is to a dog.

A smile is a curve that sets everything straight.

A smile creates:

<u>S</u>o

<u>M</u>uch

<u>I</u>mprovement with

<u>L</u>ittle

<u>E</u>ffort

Jest for the Health of It

If smiling makes us happy, laughing should make us ecstatic.

Indeed, the growing body of research on smiles fits right in with what scientists have already learned about the physiological benefits of laughter. In study after study, these facts emerge:

- ❀ A hearty laugh increases the depth of breathing, thus exercising the respiratory muscles.
- ❀ Oxygen flows into the blood and is increased, stimulating and benefiting the heart and the entire circulatory system.
- ❀ Laughter raises levels of endorphins, a pain-killing chemical released by the brain. This creates a temporarily higher pain threshold.
- ❀ Laughter also reduces pain by distracting attention from it and changing our expectations.
- ❀ After you calm down, the pulse rate drops below normal and your skeletal muscles become deeply relaxed. The stress load is lightened.

Summing up the body benefits, laughter causes:

- ❀ increased heart rate
- ❀ reduced tension
- ❀ muscle stimulation
- ❀ muscle relaxation
- ❀ increased alertness
- ❀ a temporarily higher pain threshold.

In a nutshell:
She who laughs ... lasts.

In other words, laughter gives your heart and lungs a deep-breathing workout comparable to that of aerobic exercise. Your muscles vibrate as if they've had an internal massage.

Norman Cousins likened the physiological and psychological effects to "inner jogging." I love knowing this, because I love to laugh and I do not like to jog. I have never seen a smiling jogger. Whenever I pass one pounding the pavement, I say to myself, "You go ahead and exercise the out-side of your body; I'll focus on the in-side of mine."

Picture yourself laughing. Your chest heaves, your stomach shakes, even your face, arms and legs get a workout!

In contrast, think about how you look and feel when you're stressed. Your muscles tense, your shoulders hunch up and your face tightens. Smiling and laughing relaxes these muscles, producing the opposite effects.

The United States Department of Health and Human Services ranks work-related stress as one of the five most critical threats to American health. My message is: if you take yourself too seriously, you may wind up seriously ill.

Laughter is the most efficient, economical device we have for de-stressing ourselves. It requires no elaborate equipment, spandex clothing or fancy athletic shoes. It needs no prescription and has no harmful side effects. It's always within reach.

John F. Kennedy said:

"There are three things that are real — God, human folly and laughter. The first two are beyond comprehension. So, we must do what we can with the third."

Laughter and Tears: A Continuum

The eyes, those "windows of the soul," brighten and sparkle when we laugh. This is caused by moisture created by the tear glands. Most of us can remember times we've "laughed until we cried." The release of tears is cleansing and cathartic. The AAAAHHHH after a good hearty laugh and the wiping away of tears feels wonderful.

The ability to shed emotional tears is one of the few physiological functions that separates humans from other animals. But all tears are not the same. "Science can now distinguish physiologically between reflex tears (stirred, for example, by onions) and emotional tears (arising mainly from grief or joy)," according to Smithsonian scholars.

In his book *Crying: the Mystery of Tears*, William H. Frey explains that emotional tears have a higher concentration of protein. The tears that result from sadness play an important part in removing harmful chemicals in the body that are produced by stress. They discharge the tension that accompanies sadness. Tears of laughter serve the same function.

Just as there are gender differences in various aspects of humor, there are gender differences in crying. Frey found that women cry four times more often than men, and are more likely to shed tears. When men do cry, it is less obvious. Three-quarters of the males' crying episodes in Frey's study consisted of watery eyes only.

To conduct one phase of his research, Frey sent his male and female subjects, test tubes in hand, to various sad movies, for the purpose of collecting tears for his chemical analysis. This experiment proved another hypothesis: that people cry more easily in groups. The film *All Mine to Give* was the champion tearjerker, eliciting tears from 70 percent of Frey's subjects.

Nineteen centuries ago, the Roman poet Horace wrote:

"As man laughs with those who laugh,

So he weeps with those that weep;

If thou wish me to weep,

Thou must first shed tears thyself;

Then thy sorrows will touch me."

In *All Mine To Give*, the audience often cried when the movie characters cried.

When William Frey speaks to audiences about his research, he emphasizes that crying is a healthy, normal human function. Too often people hold back tears for fear of looking childish or out of control. Instead, we should recognize that tears are beneficial and cathartic. As Charles Dickens' character Mr. Bumble stated in *Oliver Twist*, "It opens the lungs, washes the countenance, exercises the eyes and softens the temper. So cry away!"

Mood Swings

Most people assume that emotions occur spontaneously, that joy and sadness happen to us, triggered by outside events. But that's not entirely true. The essence of emotion is feeling. Feeling is an active verb. Feeling is something we do, not something that is done to us.

The truth is, humor in our lives is very much a matter within our control. The late University of Michigan psychologist James V. McConnell trained people to smile more simply by getting them to count the number of times they smiled in, say, a 10-minute period. Then he asked them to increase that number by one or two smiles, and plotted their progress on a graph.

"The learning goes even faster if one can make a videotape recording of the learning itself. Then the person has an objective measure of how frequently he or she smiles, and also how others respond to the smiles," McConnell reported. The results are very reinforcing.

Just as facial expressions alter our moods, they can also affect our memories. James Laird, a professor of psychology at Clark University in Massachusetts, says when we are angry we dwell on the negative things that make us angry. In a good mood, we remember more positive things.

We can smile when we choose to; we can concentrate on positive aspects of our lives; we can cry when the emotional release is necessary, and we can certainly create more opportunities for humor and laughter.

James McConnell compared frowns to "a type of psycho-pollution that are as deadly as smoke fumes or mercury in the drinking water. We legislate against polluted air and water," he pointed out. "Maybe we should pass a law to increase smiling, to improve mental health!"

Scientists will probably continue to debate the benefits of smiles and laughter, and whether, with respect to happiness, they are cause or effect. But no one questions their importance. And the more we can experience of both, the merrier!

CHAPTER EIGHT

HUMOR AND HEALTH CARE

OR

HO HO HOLISTIC HEALTH

Come with me on a tour of the Humor Room at General Community Hospital. The walls are brightly painted in outrageously cheerful colors. The furniture is comfortable and home-like. Flowering plants and balloon bouquets are perched near the sunny window.

From the entrance you can see a player piano along one wall with a large supply of piano roll music. In the sound-proofed audio/video nook you can watch video cassettes of Candid Camera, I Love Lucy and Laugh-In, or listen to classic radio shows like Groucho Marx and Jack Benny. The magazine racks and bookshelves are stacked with cartoon books, humor anthologies, puzzles and games.

The bulletin board is festooned with cartoons and comic strips, with announcements of humor workshops and performances by clowns, mimes, magicians and other entertainers. These performances are scheduled both in the Humor Room and selected patient areas.

A bentwood hat rack is draped with a feather boa and playful hats ranging from sombreros to bowler derbies and a flapper cloche. The toy bin is filled with yo-yos, silly putty, balloons, bubble soap and wind-up toys.

Volunteers eagerly offer to staff the Humor Room. They dress in wildly inventive headgear and colorful vests and welcome the patients and their families as well as the hospital staff. This room is designed for anyone in need of boosted spirits in the midst of their visit, workday or hospital stay.

Cancer support group meetings are held here as are Hospice programs.

Ethics committees may choose to hold sessions in this setting.

Families of patients will have use of this room to celebrate birthdays, anniversaries or role days together in a cheerful environment.

A Humor Room is such an easy, inexpensive way to bring cheer and sunshine into a somber, bland environment. Although this specific room is imaginary, variations are beginning to appear in innovative health care institutions across the country. One of my goals is to see them become as common as gift shops.

And Humor Rooms are only one example of ways we can "lighten up" the serious business of health care.

RX For Comic Relief

People have always valued humor. Humor for health improvement is not a new prescription. The ancient Greeks included a visit to "the home of comedians" for patients in their healing centers. Depictions of mirth, jokes and slapstick can be found among the Egyptian hieroglyphics.

And the Bible noted:

"A merry heart doeth good like a medicine; but a broken spirit drieth the bones." (Proverbs 17:22)

Much of the recent interest in the therapeutic effects of humor can be credited to former Saturday Review editor Norman Cousins and his 1979 book, *Anatomy of an Illness as Perceived by the Patient.*

Cousins had been diagnosed with ankylosing spondylitis, an uncommon, painful, life-threatening disease of the connective tissue. Facing chances of recovery said to be one in 500, Cousins embarked on a home remedy that included heavy doses of laughter. If negative feelings could cause imbalances in the endocrine system, he reasoned, positive feelings could reverse the process.

Bombarding himself with classic Candid Camera clips and Marx Brothers and Laurel and Hardy films, Cousins found that 10 minutes of hearty belly laughter could bring him at least two hours of pain-free, medication-free sleep.

An example of Cousins' sense of humor: During his hospital stay his breakfast tray arrived at the same time as an empty urine specimen bottle. Feeling playful, he poured his breakfast apple juice into the urine specimen bottle. When the lab technician arrived to collect the specimen, he looked at the bottle, remarking, "It looks a little cloudy today, Mr. Cousins." With a twinkle in his eye, Cousins said, "I agree, and think it needs to be put through again." And he drank the contents of the specimen bottle!

Laughter —Natural Stress Management

Patients aren't the only ones who need humor in the health care environment. While many work settings are stressful, hospitals, clinics, nursing homes and other short-term and extended care facilities are even more so. And the stress affects everyone:

- ❀ Patients are scared, anxious and embarrassed.
- ❀ Patients' families share these emotions, compounded by feelings of helplessness.
- ❀ Staff members are under constant pressure and an ever-present threat of failure. They are frustrated by their inability to relieve these sufferings completely.

Normal social conventions are suspended in this environment. People in various states of dress and undress are poked, prodded and publicly discussed. The ability to find humor in life's incongruities is vital to good mental health.

Being able to laugh at ourselves in uncomfortable situations goes a long way toward relieving the discomfort. At least for the moment, it replaces worry with optimism.

A friend went to her gynecologist's office for an examination. She was on the table with feet in the stirrups and was very tense. Then she looked at the ceiling and noticed a cheerful mobile of babies at play. She smiled and immediately felt more relaxed.

A friend tells the story of her mother's preoperative experience. When the orderly arrived to take the tense, anxious woman to the operating room, he announced with a nod toward the gurney, "I have my limousine just outside your door, and I'm here to give you curbside service." Her mother's tension, indeed the whole family's dissolved in the warmth of his humor.

Prior to "How Are You?"

Physicians and other hospital staff can play a key role in fostering a positive outlook. The same is true for professional caregivers in nursing homes and other extended care facilities and for family caregivers in the home.

Staff and other visitors often enter the patient or resident's room with too serious a facial expression. Sometimes not even establishing eye contact but peering at the medical chart, the doctor or nurse asks, "How are you feeling?" (Or worse, the more patronizing "How are we feeling today?")

The patient usually responds directly with a detailed description of ailments and complaints. No wonder physicians, nurses, aides, social workers and chaplains tell me there's little light-hearted conversation in the healthcare workplace! Visualize this scene more like a social visit. For example:

Knock. Ask permission to enter the room.

SMILE.

Say hello, and make eye contact.

Perhaps start out with a cheerful bit of personal news:

"I heard the funniest thing on television last night."

"I saw the first rose in my garden today."

"My grandson is visiting and watched me shave this morning. His father (my son-in-law) uses an electric razor. My grandson asked, "Grandpa, why do you put whipped cream on your face?"

All this might precede the necessary:

"How are you feeling today?"

You can elicit a positive response by asking the patient to respond with some bit of good news. Suggest he or she look for something amusing — a cartoon, a quote, a poem or a funny story — to share with you on your next visit. Encourage patients to look for humor, so that humor will find them.

The emphasis in medical care always seems to be on what hurts, what's wrong and where's the problem. Divert attention to the positive by asking "What is working best today?" You'll likely be able to share a smile over the response!

Finally, when you leave to continue your rounds, don't forget to say "good-bye."

Exchanging pleasantries softens the formality of a medical consultation and builds rapport between doctor and patient. The information exchanged between medical staff and those in their care can be viewed as a form of everyday conversation, in which laughter and smiling should play a normal part.

Putting It Lightly

I don't mean that the health care provider should become a comedian. Doctors do look more reassuring in white coats than clown suits. But all of us can develop the art of putting things lightly, or making the occasional joke when appropriate.

"Well Mr. Sanders, you'll be able to resume your normal activities soon but you may not be able to play shortstop for the Detroit Tigers this season."

"This injection will make you feel like a kid again — getting your first bee sting."

Unpleasant procedures frequently cause tension. Thelma, an experienced nurse, usually breaks tension with this line, "Well, how do you see me — as a friend or an enema?"

While bandaging the hand of a patient who was very anxious after an injury, one creative physician assistant commented, "You're sure going to have a problem picking your nose."

After all, the goal of the doctor-patient interaction is to improve the patient's condition through virtually any means possible. Laugher and smiles can contribute to that outcome.

You might even "prescribe" that a patient watch a funny television show or movie and tell you about it on the next visit.

Finally to the old saying, "Physician, heal thyself," I would add, "Learn to laugh at thyself." A charming example occurred when a family practitioner walked into a patient's room, set down his clipboard, and knocked over the vase of flowers on the bedside stand. Looking up apologetically, he said,

"Aren't you glad I'm not your surgeon?"

A Light Touch may be the Right Touch

For visitors:

A friend of mine, hospitalized with severe pain due to a kidney stone, had to stay in the hospital until the stone passed spontaneously or surgical intervention would be necessary. In visiting him several times early in the course of his hospital stay I noticed he was getting depressed about not passing the stone naturally. On my next visit, I had the perfect present for him! I found a large smooth stone in the park and beautifully gift wrapped it in a jeweler's ring box. I presented it to him saying, "If you can't produce one yourself — cheat!" He laughingly accepted the stone — and the next day he presented it to his doctor. There was a lot of smiling and bantering about the gift wrapped stone and a more lighthearted mood prevailed.

For patients to health care staff:

One very cheerful, but sick patient had a perfect comment for her doctor after a long, long stint in his waiting room. The doctor greeted her with an apology for having kept her waiting so long. Her reply was, "That's okay Doctor Smith — I really didn't mind waiting, but I was hopeful that you would be able to see my disease in the early stages!"

Another lighthearted patient decided to cheer her doctor a bit — she sent him a "Thank You for Getting Me Well" card. This simple act generated enormous pleasure for both parties.

Laughter Rx: Take as Directed

I suggest physicians and other health care professionals use "Humor Prescriptions." On their prescription pads I encourage them to write out (in legible handwriting!) one or more of the following:

- ❀ Please watch one funny movie or television show before our next visit.
- ❀ Please bring in a copy of a cartoon or comic strip you enjoy — or

that made you laugh.

   ❀ Would you please share a story, a joke or the funniest thing that happened to you on your next visit?

Health care is serious business. But laughing and smiling can be part of any business, no matter how serious. They may just be the lubrication that keeps things running smoothly.

Examining the Funny Bone

Hospitals are designed for emergencies, crises and acute care. Patients are "in sicker and out quicker." Extended care facilities such as nursing homes offer an opportunity to get to know the residents on a more personal basis, and to build humor and laughter into long-term relationships.

Health professionals always take a medical history. A "humor history" may help you learn more about the people you are caring for. Knowing who and what makes them laugh or smile improves your understanding and appreciation of that person. It increases opportunities for sharing and exchanging bits of humor with them. If you knew the type of humor they relate to —satire, irony, deprecation, exaggeration — you could adapt the way you talk to them about symptoms and medication. All parties benefit!

Humor history questions might include:

   ❀ Would you rather tell a joke or hear a joke?

   ❀ Who makes you laugh or smile?

❀ What role did humor play in your family as you were growing up?
❀ Do you have a favorite funny story?
❀ Do you read the comic strips? Who do you like best?
❀ Are you ticklish?
❀ Who are your favorite entertainers or performers?
❀ Do you like to make others laugh?

Being aware of what brings a person enjoyment helps in planning light-hearted activities, decorating a room, and choosing surprise gifts. Even something as simple as a cartoon on a breakfast tray can brighten a day!

Caregivers have discovered that many elderly people with dementia who are unable to remember the names of spouses or children can often sing an amusing old song from beginning to end and get enormous pleasure from it. Humor can pierce the language comprehension barriers of people who are severely sick or mentally impaired.

Residents who may be chronically ill or physically or mentally disabled may still maintain a deep sense of pleasure and affection, and the ability to express it.

Special events and celebrations can be an integral part of the extended care setting, transforming a boring, predictable or stressful environment to one that is more fun for staff and residents alike. Birthday parties are a common example!

Here are some other suggestions:

❀ Classic film fests
❀ Tapes of old time radio programs
❀ Slide shows (featuring residents and staff)
❀ Singalongs and other musical performances
❀ Birdfeeders placed where they can be easily seen
❀ Indoor and outdoor gardens
❀ Children's visiting days
❀ Pet shows
❀ Dancing and rhythmic moving to music
❀ Baby picture contests

97

Mirth Aid

One aide in a residential facility for Alzheimer's patients had a lively collection of hats, from straw sunhats and baseball caps to elegant Victorian headgear. A program called "An Evening of Modeling Hats" had the men and women residents trying on hats of all shapes and sizes. It was a memorable evening of playfulness, reminiscence and most of all, shared, spontaneous laughter.

Too often, we allow a person's medical condition to dominate all social interaction. We tend to forget that hospital patients and nursing home residents are people, not just personifications of their medical condition or disease.

Humor may help people come to terms with painful problems. Martha, an obese older woman nursing home resident suffered from pain in the stump remaining after her right leg was amputated. One day she was sitting in her wheelchair with her amputated stump visible, feeling unhappy and sorry for herself. A cheerful nurse's aide passed by and said, "Hello Martha, nice to see you — how are the ballet lessons coming along?" Martha smiled and then laughed and so did many of the other residents in the TV room. Within a few seconds Martha said, "Wait until you see me in my new tutu!"

An exchanged smile or a shared chuckle help remind us of our common interests and help bring all parties in the health care setting closer together.

Visitors Welcome

Dorothy Coons, project director for The University of Michigan Institute of Gerontology, edited the book, *A Better Life,* aimed at helping family members, volunteers and staff improve quality of life for nursing home residents suffering from Alzheimer's Disease and related disorders.

She points out that "visiting" in this setting is more than a matter of polite conversation. Linking a resident's past life with the present helps them maintain their identity. Especially as an Alzheimer's patient is less able to communicate verbally, the family and other visitors need to focus on shared

experiences and activities to help their loved one stay invol
around her or him.

Variety, special events, companionship, special pla
surely tone are ingredients that add up to successful nursing home visits.

Home-Brewed Remedies

Anyone can use humor to help lighten up the serious business of illness.

When a friend was hospitalized for an extended period with leukemia, a group of us helped overcome the discomfort and listlessness produced by monthly doses of chemotherapy. We regularly brought inexpensive items to transform her fundamental hospital room to a more fun-filled room. How?

- ❀ We changed her window "view" each month with posters of cityscapes, mountains, oceans and palm trees.
- ❀ We hung a home made mobile with pictures of her pets over her bed, and brought in a goldfish bowl for her night stand.
- ❀ We reinstated her normal social role of hostess by filling a big basket with a changing array of daily treats, from chocolate kisses to fresh strawberries to home baked cookies. These she could offer to visitors and staff.
- ❀ We kept her entertained and buoyant with a steady stream of comic books, balloons and toys.

The hospital staff told us she handled her chemotherapy much better than expected. Our action required creativity, but very little money.

Our efforts also boosted the spirits of the doctors, nursing staff, visitors and other patients, who never knew what new surprises to expect when they entered the room. As I've mentioned, humor benefits health professionals as much as their patients!

The same principle applies to caregivers in the home environment. Several of us had been concerned about a woman we knew who was caring for her seriously ill husband. She was afraid to leave the house for fear that omething might happen to him while she was gone. But her constant vigilance was taking a toll on her health.

We pooled our resources to give our friend the most useful gift we could think of: time for herself. We took turns staying with her husband, and gave her a choice of such options as seeing a movie, having her hair done, having lunch in a restaurant or going for a swim.

For the last bit of reassurance, we bought her a beeper. She was finally able to permit herself some relaxation, knowing that she could be contacted immediately in case of an emergency.

This outreach of friendship, support and help was offered with a genuine desire to help lighten up this most stressful period. The lighthearted activities we shared permitted some opportunities for laughter or silliness (something funny in the movie, the frivolous act of having a pedicure) — and laughter is like a mini-vacation from reality. Thinking and creating and sharing in positive experiences with our friend helped us all to be more refreshed, renewed friends and caregivers.

A Good Prognosis

Humor has a positive impact on health from any and all perspectives — it assists patients, care providers, visitors, family and friends. It diminishes stress and restores hope and optimism. Laughter is not a cure for anything — humor should be a part of an overall treatment plan, not a substitute for medical attention.

Erma Bombeck's 1989 book, *I Want To Grow Hair, I Want To Grow Up, I Want*

100

To Go to Boise, is about children with cancer, and the optimism with which they triumph over their illness. It is one of the finest testimonies to the power of humor on health. Few people believed that humor and cancer could be a compatible topic. As one of the kids Bombeck interviewed asked, "Would you be happier if we cried all the time?"

She quotes a letter from a mother that reads: "Humor is what got all of us through the clinic visits, the hospital stays, the blood tests, the loss of hair and weight. There is always something on the light side if you look for it

Humor is one of the healthiest most therapeutic mechanisms that human beings have. Humor and laughter are healing physically and emotionally. Humor prompts laughter; laughter provides the biochemical change.

Humor is great in health care. I still can't figure out why Blue Cross doesn't pay for it!

Humor in Counseling

"A person without a sense of humor is like a wagon without springs—jolted by every pebble in the road." —Henry Ward Beecher

Laughter — a wonderful coping mechanism

Humor may be used in counseling with wonderful benefits for both client and therapist. Sometimes exaggerating problems may help put them in proportion. "So how many big crises did you bring in today?" asked one social worker of a client. Smiling, the therapist continued, "One million, ten million?" The client started to laugh and responded, "At least ten million" — and then they both relaxed and started in on the session.

Many people do not use humor in the course of their daily lives, and as a result are probably not familiar and knowledgeable about how to use it appropriately. A wise counselor/therapist may gently initiate humor by joking about general topics such as the weather to encourage a more lighthearted relationship and prompt the patient to use humor independently.

One counselor who uses humor as a part of treatment has a "magic wand" (a silver sequinned cardboard model) in her office. When a client says, "I wish I could," she hands them the wand and waits to see what happens. Frequently, a smile or laughter is the result and a shift of attitude — a more playful one — takes place.

Support groups are a wonderful way of coping with the demands of problems facing us. In these groups, people find out that their problems are not unique, that others have lived and worked through similar situations and used approaches and strategies you hadn't thought about. One of the most marvelous parts of a support group is the safety of sharing with people who have experienced the same stress and strain. AND, naturally humor frequently pops its cheerful head within these groups.

Example from the Well Spouse Foundation newsletter. "My husband calls me all the time. 'Helen! Helen! Do this, Helen!' I've figured out how to solve my problem. I'm going to change my name." While this example might not strike a non-caregiver as being very humorous, another caregiver can benefit greatly from this light exchange.

Nancy, 31 years old and recently widowed, discovered that the only place she felt safe laughing was in her Young Widow's Support Group. Attending the monthly meetings was the bright spot she eagerly looked forward to. "This is the only place where I'm able to laugh about the unlaughable. It took me a long time to let myself go, but I know without the laughter of the group, I wouldn't have started to heal."

Elaine, a 60 year old psychologist, is an active member of a breast cancer self-help group. The most bonding thing she did for the group was to name it Bosom Buddies. Their first social event sported BYOB (or not!) on the invitation. We grow up the first day we have a good laugh...at ourselves!

A good therapist establishes a safe and secure environment for the client, creating places where people feel free to both cry and to laugh.

Stress the Positive!

People in therapy take themselves very seriously. The patient may have many serious problems, yet with guidance may be able to see another side and a different perspective through a lighthearted exchange with the therapist. Many therapists feel that there is no better way to say "You are okay,

102

and the sky isn't falling and I can see other sides to you besides an unhappy sick person." Nobody ever was taught that getting better can't be fun!

When a person becomes stressed and anxious, her focus becomes more narrow, less creative. She is easily angered. Humor allows her to cognitively reframe a situation and examine the problem from another perspective

Rollo May said, "Humor is the healthy way of feeling a distance between one's self and the problem, a way of standing off and looking at one's problem with perspective."

Eight Warning Signs of Good Mental Health

1. Persistent presence of support network.
2. Persistent sense of humor.
3. Tendency to adapt to changing conditions.
4. Persistent sense of humor.
5. Willingness to communicate feelings.
6. Persistent sense of humor.
7. Increased appetite for physical activity.
8. Persistent sense of humor.

If several of these indicators are present, you may be at risk for mental wellness.

Medical Terminology For the Layman

Artery — The study of fine paintings.
Barium — What you do when CPR fails.
Cesarean Section — A district in Rome.
Colic — A sheep dog
Coma — A punctuation mark.
Congenital — Friendly.
Dilate — To live long
Fester— Quicker.

103

G.I Series — Baseball games between teams of soldiers.

Grippe — A suitcase.

Hangnail — A coat hook.

Medical Staff — A doctor's cane.

Minor Operation — Coal digging.

Morbid — A higher offer.

Nitrate — Lower than the day rate.

Node — Was aware of

Organic — Musical.

Outpatient — A person who has fainted.

Post-operative — A letter carrier.

Protein — In favor of young people.

Secretion — Hiding anything.

Serology — Study of English knighthood.

Tablet — A small table.

Tumor — An extra pair.

Urine — Opposite of you're out.

Varicose Veins — Blood vessels which are very close together.

Chapter Nine

Humor and Aging

or

Laughter and Years

int to be thoroughly used up when I die, for the harder I work, the more I live. I rejoice in life for its own sake. Life is no "brief candle" for me. It is a sort of a splendid torch, which I have got hold of for the moment; and I want to make it burn as brightly as possible before handing it on to future generations." —George Bernard Shaw.

I consider myself somewhat of an expert on aging because I've been doing it for the past 64 years. What bothers me is that all I read and hear about are the problems and concerns of aging. We begin to age the minute we are born — and the process doesn't stop until we die. Aging is part of our life span. Research confirms that aging is not a disease. Growing old isn't so bad, especially if you consider the alternative!

There is good news and bad news about aging: the good news is that aging is looking a lot better than it used to. The bad news is that we're going to die someday. The good news is that someday — thanks to the wonders of science and healthy living habits — is being pushed farther and farther into the future. The bad news is that we're still going to die someday. Yes, we all age, some slowly, some rapidly. What we can control is the way we choose to deal with the losses and changes that come with the aging process. Aging would indeed be gray and grim without a good belly laugh frequently. Each day we live is an extension of a gift. So while we're living, let's look at some good news about aging.

Those Who Laugh...Last!

In spite of the many negative attitudes towards aging presented in jokes, stories and especially birthday cards, there are positives as well. This is an age and a stage to start pleasing ourselves. One of the many advantages of aging is no longer caring what other people think. Being comfortable with who we are is a major shift in our thinking and perspective. I have often felt that we all start out in life without an "Owner's Manual" to guide us. It's a bit like spending the first 50 years or so driving with a Learner's Permit and suddenly you get your license to drive this body, and chart your way.

Another blessing of maturity is that time, which represents the gift of life, is no longer a commodity to be squandered thoughtlessly. Many older adults are happy to give up boring meetings, dinner parties — even friends — they no longer enjoy. We study for pleasure now — not for grades. At last people give themselves permission to luxuriate in the slowed pace of just listening to music as a single activity, not trying to accomplish three tasks at the same time. Walking on a beach may take up half a day, and beach walking memories can be stored up for future days. Grandchildren — those delightful links to the past and future — often provide relaxed, fun-filled shared activities. Older people experiment with new lifestyles and innovative living arrangements. In later years many of us become more courageous and resourceful and playful than ever before. Past events in our lives which were embarrassing or possibly even dangerous, may now be our treasured funny stories. Tragedy plus time equals comedy...or someday you'll laugh about this. Someday has arrived! When faced with trying problems, try to step back and see the humorous side of the situation.

Aging is a matter of perspective. To illustrate what I mean by "perspective," consider this case history presented to a class of graduate nurses studying psychological aspects of aging.

"The patient is a white female. She neither speaks nor comprehends the spoken word. Sometimes she babbles incoherently for hours on end. She is disoriented about person, place and time. I have worked with her for about six months but she still does not recognize me.

"She shows complete disregard for her physical appearance and makes no effort to assist in her own care. She must be fed, clothed and bathed by others. Because she is toothless, her food must be pureed. Because she is incontinent, she must be changed and bathed often.

"Her sleep pattern is erratic. Often she awakens in the middle of the night. Her screaming wakes others. Most of the time she is quite happy, but several times a day she becomes quite agitated without apparent cause..."

Various nurses admitted that caring for such a patient would make them feel frustrated or even hopeless. Then the doctor passed around the photo of the patient. It was his six-month-old daughter.

Recapture a spirit of playfulness and silliness

I'm not talking about being childish, but childlike. There are many childlike qualities that serve us well all our lives, but may diminish as we get older.

- ❀ Curiosity
- ❀ Playfulness
- ❀ Willingness to experiment
- ❀ Flexibility
- ❀ Imaginativeness
- ❀ Open-mindedness

Here's a quick self-analysis exercise to get you thinking about childlike qualities:

1. List the three best characteristics of your personality as a child or younger person.
2. Play around with these and put them in priority order — which one do you consider the most valuable.
3. Write down a few ways you might be able to recapture any of these characteristics.
4. Does the fear of appearing foolish stifle your enthusiasm or curiosity?
5. Do you ever find yourself thinking about what "THEY" would think? Who is the "THEY" and why do you care about "THEM"?
6. Draw two circles on a sheet of paper. The first circle represents your waking world for the past week. Now draw a pie-shaped wedge in this circle representing play and lighthearted activity, amusement or pleasure. The second circle on your page repre-

sents your fantasy week — if you could create any type of activity for the next week — draw a pie-shaped wedge to represent what you would like your fantasy week to look like. Now — what do you need to do to make your fantasy week come true? This is your prescription for play — TAKE AS DIRECTED!

You don't stop laughing because you grow old; you grow old because you stop laughing!

Bernie Siegel, the author and physician, said, "As I grow older, I come to realize that life is inherently disorderly. Now I know that living well means forgetting about rigid schedules and "To Do" lists. It means learning to find happiness, fulfillment and tranquillity in face of disorder.

Don't Retire Your Sense of Humor!

A sense of humor is your best tool to keep the nuisance of aging in perspective. It's tempting to dwell on the down side. Often when older people congregate at meals and other social events, they spend most of the evening hashing over their various chronic health problems. My advice: put a three-minute time limit on the discussion of aches and pains. Then spend the next three minutes talking about what feels good! When you pay a visit to someone elderly, move swiftly from "How are you feeling?" to upbeat questions: "What was the best thing you had to eat this week?" "What did you enjoy most on television?" Or ask questions intended to stir happy memories: "Tell me about the first car you owned." "Who was the first person you ever kissed?" "What's the funniest thing that ever happened to you?" Presenting older people with a chance to cuddle a puppy or kitten or watch two-year-olds at play are two more ways to lift their spirits. Aging happens to our bodies, but the mind can continue to grow. Even if you just found the coffee pot in the fridge. Let loose and laugh at yourself. Humor prevents hardening of the attitudes. Enjoy life! This is NOT a dress rehearsal!

109

Hot Flash or Power Surge?

Menopause isn't exactly a big giggle, but we can be lighthearted about some things. Barbara, a 48 year old salesclerk was always cold. She dreaded getting up on freezing cold nights to go down a long hall to an even colder bathroom. Then her hot flashes started—and all of a sudden , it was easier for her to leave her warm bed. She eagerly shared her positive attitude with younger friends, telling them that hot flashes were "cool"!

My mother was good role model for menopausal mirth. Her maiden name was Gordon and her nickname was Flash Gordon. She and her friends were all card players. I remember coming home from school and seeing my mother's beautifully dressed friends playing cards. My mother, also dressed beautifully , but topless was a sight to behold. She always played cards wearing a skirt, hat perched jauntily on her head and topless. Firmly entrenched in her steel ribbed brassiere and sporting a cotton scarf around her neck was her concession to frequent hot flashes. She was also known to remark, "I'm so glad hot flashes don't make noise!" Flash Gordon would not let changing estrogen levels keep her sense of humor from shining through!

Keeping your sense of humor during the mood swings you encounter is one of the best things you can do for yourself. Absence of humor is one of the first signs of feeling depressed. Research has shown that when someone can start laughing again, it is one of the first signs of emotional stability. In other words, one of the warning signs of health may be a persistent sense of humor. George Burns said, "Age is a case of mind over matter. If you don't mind, it doesn't matter!"

The Ageless Spirit—the Playful Spirit

In spite of the normal losses of aging, older people are coping by laughing. The use of humor by older adults reduces anxieties, fears, depression and paves the way to adaptation and acceptance of limitations. It also can give seniors a hopeful perspective and the strength to survive.

Fred, a crusty 89-year-old New Englander, loved having people ask him the "How are you?" question. His standard answer was always, "Can't complain — (l-o-n-g pause for maximum effect) and then the punchline: "Sure like to, though."

Sam Green, my father-in-law lived into his 90's. His favorite joke (which he told us hundreds of times!) was the following. Three things happen to you as you get older. The first is that you start to forget things…and I can't remember the other two!

Lola, an active older woman, failed her driver's license renewal exam. Instead of being depressed, she bartered her baking skills for her neighbor's driving skills and everyone is happy. Lola says, "I can't merge… but I'm still living in the fast lane!"

Molly, a cheerful 79 year old friend, claims she is living in the hereafter. She plays around with her forgetfulness. Every time she goes upstairs to fetch something, she asks herself, "Now what I am here after?"

Another approach to forgetfulness is the mantra used by Pearl, a lighthearted 72 year old social worker. "I knew it once… I'll know it again… I just don't remember it now!"

The "I Must Act My Age" Mentality

Many people refuse to take part in lighthearted activities because they believe they've outgrown such "foolishness." They say things such as "She should know better than to try to be a tapdancer at her age!" Or they refuse to join the egg toss at picnics. Remember, bicycles, swings, roller skates come in all sizes. Get rid of your fun-block!

In her newest book, *Fountain of Age*, Betty Friedan says, "I am myself at this age. It took me all these years to put the missing pieces together, to confront my own age in terms of integrity and generativity, moving into the unknown future with comfort now, instead of being stuck in the past. I have never felt so free."

Don't postpone joy!

"Vanity" by Elise Maclay demonstrates a playful lighthearted approach to aging:

111

VANITY

I used to hate it so
When a new wrinkle appeared,
Creasing my forehead,
Dragging down my mouth,
Marring my cheek.
I used to sit in front of the mirror
Stretching the skin taut with my fingers,
I could lift it and smooth it,
Which didn't make me feel better,
It made me feel worse, remembering how beautiful I used to be.
Well, pretty.
But lately, for almost a year, maybe,
Looking in the mirror hasn't been such a shock.
Am I getting used to it?
Am I reconciled?
Has the deterioration slowed?
No. I need new glasses.
What a joke.
My eyesight's deteriorating faster than my face.

A lighthearted approach to all stages of life will give you a more positive outlook. Remember, time flies whether you're having fun or not!

112

Chapter Ten

Bits and Pieces

Leftovers and Planned Overs

Laughs, But not Least

Party invitations tend to come in packages of 8, 10 or 12. Friends rarely come in neat multiples of these numbers. If you're like me, you've got a drawer full of odds and ends, three invitations to a Football Tailgate Party; two to a birthday bash. A few years ago, I merged my assortment of leftover invitations to children's birthday parties and other celebrations and invited friends to a "Leftover Potluck." Each guest brought leftovers from the freezer and fridge — turkey hash from last Thanksgiving; warmed-over pot roasts and sliced pizza. Everyone enjoyed the eclectic meal and appreciated the freed-up freezer space. I like leftovers. Some people throw away that last bit of chicken or spoonful of vegetables. I squirrel it away in the freezer (Depression mentality strikes again!) to be later added to a hearty soup or chowder.

Over the years I had amassed thick files of ideas, anecdotes, examples and data on how humor relates to work, health and families. Most of my material sorted itself easily into these broad chapter headings. But I found there were "leftovers" — bits and pieces that didn't quite fit into the categories but are nonetheless worthy of inclusion. So I offer you my chapter of leftovers — a picnic of potluck "yucks." They are further evidence of the myriad ways humor touches all parts of our lives.

Humor and Women or
Mona Lisa's Secret

Humor touches women in the same way as men. But do we laugh at the same things? Are the rules different? If you were to take an informal poll of your friends and co-workers and ask each of them to tell a joke, I'll bet the men you approach would be able to come up with one on the spot. Women are more apt to reply, "I'm no good at telling jokes." Or, "I can never remember them." One reason is that we've had less practice. The joke teller in a group commands the center of attention, and many women are more comfortable away from that limelight. We're trained to be "good listeners." In fact, the woman who is the true "life of the party," reeling off one-liners, runs the risk of being labeled loud and obnoxious.

114

You've probably heard this one:
A guy goes to his doctor for a checkup and the doctor says,
"You've got six months to live."
The patient says, "I want a second opinion."
The doctor says, "Okay. You're also ugly."

Can you imagine a woman telling this story? Women's humor is rarely crude or cruel. It doesn't center around bathroom activities, sexual acts or their mothers-in-law. Ours has a softer edge. Women usually are story tellers, not joke tellers.

Consider some of our most prominent women humor writers. Jean Kerr, Peg Bracken, Judith Viorst and especially Erma Bombeck are writers who find humor in the mundane cycle of daily events and family relationships. Compare the cartoon strips of "Beetle Bailey" and "Cathy." Beetle is always goofing off or getting beat up by Sarge. Cathy frets about dating, dieting and keeping up with the laundry.

Is there a woman alive who doesn't relate to Cathy's frustration in trying on swimsuits?

Today's comediennes are changing the image of comic women. "Lucy" ruled the air waves in the 50s, but today, we rarely see Lily Tomlin playing the bimbo or engaging in slapstick.

If I offered you, dear reader, $100 to tell me a father-in-law joke, do you think you'd win the bet? Would I be foolish enough to make the same offer for a mother-in-law joke? For years, women have been the butt of many jokes. There has been a recent rash of dumb blonde jokes. They've broken out on the face of America like zits at a high school prom.

Q: How can you tell if a dumb blonde has used the computer?
A: There's white-out on the screen.

or

Q: How do you make a blonde laugh on Monday?
A: Tell her a joke on Friday.

If these jokes sound vaguely familiar, it may be because they were once told as

115

a (fill in your least favorite ethnic group, minority, sports team, etc.). There is no Blonde Anti-Defamation League, no National Organization of Blonde People. Blondes were thought to be the last group people can legally joke about.

Recently the American male has become the hapless butt of male-bashing gags and dumb-men jokes making the rounds of office conversations, talk shows and comedy clubs. It's been said that in a world of rights-conscious minorities, men may be the last safe target for put-down humor.

Q: What is the best way to get a man to do sit-ups?
A: Put the remote control between his toes.

or

Q: What's the difference between government bonds and men?
A: Bonds eventually mature.

or

Q: Why are all dumb blonde jokes one-liners?
A: So men can understand them.

Dumb men jokes don't pick on specific men. The jokes aren't even aimed at any of the major male subgroups — fathers, husbands, boyfriends, brothers, rich men, poor men, bald men, middle-aged men. Traditionally, most put-down jokes make fun of someone who is struggling, oppressed, downtrodden or a member of a minority or ethnic group. But dumb men jokes take on ALL MEN!

Society could use more social humor — human foibles that make us see our common humanity and laugh at our troubles. If we can keep out unkind or crude humor, and remember not to laugh at — but with — people we'll all be the better for it. Humor should put us up — not down!

Women's humor is healthy and humane. There's only one place where we've been hesitant to let our hair down, according to author Barbara Mackoff, and that's in the work place. In her book, *What Mona Lisa Knew* she warns that taking yourself too seriously on the job can actually keep you from getting ahead.

"During the 'Power Pumps Era' of the 70s and 80s, corporate women donned a teeth-gritting grimness to match their monotone suits," says Mackoff.

And yet, as discussed in the chapter Humor & Work, humor forges bonds and displays creativity and flexibility.

A survey of personnel executives by Hall and Associates showed that 84 percent say people with a better sense of humor do a better job. When 200 executives were asked to name the qualities that kept women from succeeding, "lack of a sense of humor" was near the top of the list.

Women have been concentrating on perfecting their work rather than forging working alliances, Mackoff insists. "It sounds paradoxical to say that a woman has to be funny to be taken seriously. Getting in on the joke is critical."

Much notice has been paid to the "glass ceiling" that bars women from the highest executive ranks. Perhaps the sound that will shatter the glass ceiling is the sound of laughter.

Sick Humor or
How Laughter Dispels Tragedy

Moments after the space shuttle Challenger with teacher Christa McAuliffe aboard exploded in 1986, the jokes began.

"What does NASA stand for?"
"Need Another Seven Astronauts."

"What were Christa McAuliffe's last words?"
"What's this button for?"

It seems incongruous that a tragedy that generated such universal grief could also spawn humor. Yet the jokes spread rapidly through the country. They seemed cathartic, leaving a sense of relief in their wake. Just as humor serves as an antidote to personal tension and pain, so too did it help neutralize the pain of a nation.

Jerry Zolten, a speech professor at Pennsylvania State University, studied the shuttle stories. They were "a way to vent socially unacceptable material," he concluded. "Joking is a luxury, kind of like a license to communicate what we would not otherwise communicate."

117

Zolten conducted a survey of 57 adults of various ages and occupations to test their response to various forms of humor. He included one of the shuttle jokes. ("Where did the Challenger astronauts spend their winter vacation? All over Florida.") His findings illustrate the ambivalence most of us feel about sick humor. Many of those surveyed ranked the shuttle joke among the most offensive, but also rated it among the funniest and the most likely to be repeated.

Research on humor has long recognized the role of humor within even the grimmest realities of life. Nor is it a new phenomenon. People still repeat the one liner that emerged after Abraham Lincoln was assassinated at the Ford's Theater: "Aside from that Mrs. Lincoln, how did you enjoy the show?"

C. David Mortensen, Professor of Communication Arts at the University of Wisconsin, surveyed 4,500 people to learn their initial reactions to the 1981 Reagan assassination attempt. He had not expected that humor would be mentioned in so many responses.

"The respondents reported saying or hearing things like "the cowboy finally took a real bullet," Mortensen relates. Like other researchers, he concludes that such morbid remarks serve a serious purpose. It provides us with "a primitive defense against the possibility of our own death at the hands of another."

Humor even prevailed in the death camps of Nazi Germany. The diaries of the Jewish victims and survivors reveal surprisingly little gallows humor and a sense of persistent optimism.

Many of the jokes portray small victories at Nazi expense. Others anticipated the end of Nazi reign. For example this one, in which Hitler consults an astrologer to find out when he will die. "On a Jewish holiday," he is told. "Yes but which Jewish holiday?" he demands. The reply is: "Any day you die will be a Jewish holiday!"

Steve Lipman, a writer for Jewish Week, has said, "If chicken soup is the Jewish penicillin, then I call humor the Jewish novocain." I think the statement is true, but it extends across all cultures.

Humor and Sex or
Recapture the Thrill

If someone asked you, "How's your sex life?" how would you respond. Never mind with who or how often. The real issue is — are you having fun?

If sex with your partner has become as routine as brushing your teeth, and about as inspiring, maybe it's time to stir the pot a bit. Revive your sense of adventure and bring in a spirit of play.

You remember what play is, don't you? Play is creative and spontaneous. It uses your imagination, not your intellect. Put aside "what works" and "the way we've always done it," and open your mind to some new possibilities.

Play is a process, not a goal. If your sole purpose in engaging in sex is to have an orgasm, then you're too goal-oriented. Some people are so focused on the result, they miss out on the fun that leads up to it.

It's called forePLAY for a reason!

One reason for Dr. Ruth's enormous popularity is that she gives people permission to laugh about sex!

Remember your first kiss? Maybe it was at a neighborhood game of spin the bottle or in the back seat of a car on a double date. Remember how your heart beat as it happened and the secret pleasure of replaying it over and over in your mind in the days that followed?

Now, remember the first time you had sex with your partner? Of course you do! You may not recall the day but I'll bet you can conjure up the place and time and the circumstances. I bet you can recall how you felt. This was a landmark event in your personal history.

If you think of it as history, remember, history can repeat itself!

The bedroom is a fine place for playful experimentation. Here are some things other couples do to lighten up and liven up their sex life. If some of these ideas strike you as outrageous or too off-the-wall for your tastes, that's okay. Maybe they'll stimulate some ideas of your own. First, some ground rules to consider:

- ❈ Remove the distractions. Ideally, pack the kids off for a weekend with the grandparents or check into a motel. At the very least, turn off the television (unless you've rented an X-rated film as part of the warm-up activities).

❀ Clear your mind. This is no time to worry about tomorrow's board meeting or review your to-do list. Consciously replace these thoughts with scenes from your favorite sexy movie or passage in a novel — whatever turns you on. Indulge your fantasies.

❀ Engage all of your five senses. Sexual pleasure involves seeing, touching, hearing, smell and taste.

The Loving Laughing Connection

Where does a sense of humor come in? Because it's difficult to try something new and adventurous if you're afraid of making a mistake and looking foolish. The idea here is to throw out the old rules. What's the worst that can happen? If your "experiment" is a flop and you and your partner can laugh about it, that in itself is a positive accomplishment.

Attention! Humor helps in attracting a mate! In study after study where subjects were asked to rank the qualities they most admired in a prospective mate, a sense of humor almost always was at the top of the list.

Adult relationships don't have to be predictable or unexciting. Practice random acts of novelty. Leave notes on your mate's pillow, mirror or car seat. Eat Sunday breakfast on Wednesday night. Cook a new exotic dish — together. And eat it on a blanket on the living room floor or on a card table in your bedroom. Rent a tandem bike. Have a picnic breakfast.

Think about spending a night at a Bed and Breakfast Inn. Thirty or 300 miles from home doesn't matter, it's the change of scenery and mentality that counts.

Celebrate the little things — and little nothings.

❀ I'm glad we're still together Day.

❀ I walked six miles toDay.

❀ I balanced my checkbook Day.

❀ I had yogurt instead of chocolate cake at lunch Day.

120

Sex is a form of communication and a basic pleasure that gives a profound sense of well-being. A couple can strengthen their relations and create new freedoms of sharing, laughter and love.

Does Laughter Have an Accent?
or Lost in Translation

Humor is a common language. In this rapidly changing world, people from different cultural, political, religious and socio-economic backgrounds are now living and working together. Humor is one form of communication to which almost everyone can relate. It helps erase differences between people. When people laugh together a bonding effect takes place. It is like saying, "We have something in common — we are not so different."

Laughing together can turn strangers into friends. We all need laughter to help us cope. For newcomers in foreign lands, laughter is especially welcome.

With business going global, it is important to remember the old saying about when in Rome...It is polite, kind and appreciated to know and sometimes use a few pleasant phrases of the local language. However, extreme care must be taken to assure that nothing offensive or improper is expressed. When Pepsi-Cola invaded the huge Chinese market, the product's slogan, "Come alive with the Pepsi generation," was rendered into Chinese as "Pepsi brings back your dead ancestors!"

What an American finds funny may be considered insulting or in poor taste in other countries. Americans frequently laugh in public at jokes about the United States president. It may not be accepted in some countries to laugh at the ruling leader.

Even when the language sounds the same, there may be total confusion—and humor is lost. There is the story about the Englishman on holiday in Kansas. He looked around at all the corn he saw growing. "Whatever do you do with all this corn?" he asked the farmer. "Well," said the farmer, "we eat what we can, and what we can't, we can!" And he threw back his head and laughed uproariously, which puzzled the Englishman. Upon returning to England, he told of his trip to Kansas and asking the farmer about the corn. He told his friends

121

that the farmer said, "We consume as much as we are able, that which we are unable to consume we put up in tins. And the farmer laughed and laughed, and I never found out why."

Warning! Different Jokes for Different Folks

The structured humor of jokes remains very difficult to understand. There are so many ways to miss the point of a joke. There may be a "play on words." Stereotypes of people in certain occupations, ethnic groups or relationships may be unfamiliar.

Someone at the United Nations once fed a common English saying into a translating computer. The machine was asked to translate the statement into Chinese, then into French and finally back into English. The adage chosen was "Out of sight, out of mind." What came back was "invisible insane."

Many jokes are off-color, racist, sexist, ethnic, politically incorrect and full of negative stereotypes. In addition to making people feel uncomfortable, these jokes aren't usually funny to most people from the same culture. Change the culture and jokes may be totally lost. For example, there are many jokes about male baldness in America. American men are assumed more attractive if they have a full head of hair. However, many men may have lost their hair and/or fear going bald. Asian men generally don't become bald, so there are many fewer jokes in Japan, China or Korea about baldness. In some cultures, a bald head may be considered a sign of wisdom.

Erma Bombeck's unique ability to laugh at everyday life in America such as carpools, mountains of laundry and whining kids may make no sense (not nonsense) to non-Americans.

Non-verbal humor is one excellent way to bridge the language gap. Playing peek-a-boo with a baby needs no translation and almost always elicits a smile or giggle. Magic tricks, juggling and mime are other ways to communicate in a lighthearted way.

Of all the qualities required in a foreign arena, in addition to patience, a sense of humor and cross cultural sensitivity are vital. I believe that if people can laugh together, they can learn to live together. Cross culture need not be angry!

Humor and Religion
or Let Us Play

Religion, like sex, is too often treated as a solemn, serious business. Children learn this from their first visit to a house of worship, where they are admonished to settle down and HUSH at the first giggle and squirm. Glancing about, the child tries to call attention to the lady wearing the funny hat in the next pew. This provokes more shushing, often accompanied by threats.

The child grows up with an image of the church or synagogue as a somber place, rather than a place of joy and gladness.

It is true that many religious and ethnic minorities have been persecuted. But as we saw in the previous discussion of "sick" humor, much humor comes from pain. Perhaps that's why so many comics come from ethnic backgrounds. Blacks and Jews, for example, have suffered as a group and used humor as a form of catharsis.

You may think it's stretching the point to say that a sense of humor can enhance your spiritual peacefulness. But laughter and spirituality have so very much in common. At the core of each is a willingness to play, to let go of assumptions and expectations and to open our hearts, our minds, and our souls to new possibilities.

Children are a wonderful source of wisdom. Here are some examples of kids' views of reality:

✿   Noah's wife was named Joan of Ark.

✿   The epistles are the wives of the apostles.

✿   The Fifth Commandment is "Humor thy father and mother."

In 1986, a group emerged calling itself the Fellowship of Merry Christians. Its membership now exceeds 10,000 and its message is spread through a monthly publication called "The Joyful Noiseletter." It's chock-full of clean jokes, cartoons and upbeat anecdotes that can be incorporated into sermons and church newsletters — for non-Christian congregations as well.

Many churches and synagogues are experiencing declining membership. If houses of worship are going to survive and grow, there is a need to bring a spirit of joy and celebration and good humor into the way people worship.

Martin Luther wrote, "God is not a God of Sadness, but the Devil is. It is pleasing to the dear God whenever thou rejoices or laughest from the bottom of thy heart."

Again we are reminded of the biblical quote from Proverbs 17:22:

"A merry heart doeth good like a medicine; but a broken spirit drieth the bones."

The Last Laugh
or Life Everlaughter

Woody Allen said, "I don't mind the idea of dying, I just don't want to be there when it happens."

The importance of joy and humor to our spiritual life is never more apparent than on the occasion of death.

Most of us picture funerals as sad, tearful affairs. Yet a funeral should be a celebration of the LIFE that has passed, rather than grief at its ending. In the old French Quarter of New Orleans, traffic stops to make way for a procession of Black jazz musicians playing "Just A Closer Walk With Thee." In the Irish neighborhoods of Brooklyn, a funeral is followed by a jubilant wake. Many other cultures mark death with music, banquets and other rituals that involve joy and laughter. The first three letters of the word funeral spell FUN.

When families are drawn together, even for sad occasions such as funerals, there is bound to be reminiscing and story-telling. Many family stories are funny, even if they weren't funny when they happened! Where shared laughter has always been part of the relationship, it should be part of the final farewell. As I once heard a person remark during services for a loved one, "If he could tell us how he wanted to be remembered, I think he would say we should dry our tears and smile." Jim Henson, creator of the Muppets, requested that favorite jokes be told at his funeral.

We look for opportunities to laugh at things we are afraid of. A book of cartoons called Unpleasant Ways to Die exaggerates our worst fears, permitting us to laugh. Sometimes people close to death are a source of inspiration themselves. As in this story:

A terminally ill patient looked forward to her doctor's daily rounds.

When he arrived quite late one morning, she laughed and quipped, been dying to see you."

And this:

A woman who was never married was making arrangements for her funeral, and requested all women pallbearers. Asked why, she replied: "Men never took me out when I was alive, so they're not going to take me out when I'm dead!"

Death is not a failure. It is part of a continuum, and it can be lighthearted. Personally, I would like to have my funeral be a reflection of the happiness I experienced in my life. Instead of somber music, I shall have the big band sound of Glenn Miller playing. Having suffered all my life with the label of "singing impaired," I think I might make a tape of me singing a concert of my favorite songs for such a captive audience! Instead of flowers, I wish to have helium balloons — and let them float off on the breeze at the end of my funeral service. I have chosen the menu for the reception to follow — chocolate, chocolate and yet even more chocolate! It sounds so good to me, I'm glad I'm going to be the star of the event!

There is absolutely no documentation of anyone's last words being, "I wish I'd been more serious."

As George Bernard Shaw said:

"Life does not cease to be funny when people die, just as it does not cease to be serious when people laugh."

And Finally

I leave you with these thoughts from Ralph Waldo Emerson *On the Meaning of Success:*

"To laugh often and much; to win the respect of intelligent people and the affection of children; to appreciate beauty, to find the best in others; to leave the world a bit better, whether by a healthy child, a garden patch or a redeemed social condition; to know even one life has breathed easier because you have lived. This is to have succeeded."

It is significant that the very first line emphasizes the importance of laughter. In this world, a good time to laugh is any time you can!

The End

Congratulations! You have finished this book. I sincerely hoped it has helped you make sense of humor!

If, after reading the book, you wish to share any humorous experience, or would like to contact me, please do:

Lila Green
2125 Nature Cove
Ann Arbor, MI 48104
(313) 677-1517.

In expansion of these ideas, see Chapter 10, "Humor and Lighthearted Activities" by this author in the book, *Specialized Dementia Care Units*, edited by Dorothy H. Coons (Johns Hopkins Press, 1991).

REFERENCES

Bombeck, Erma, *I Want to Grow Hair, I Want to Grow Up, I Want to Go to Boise*, Harper & Row, New York, NY, 1989.

Cousins,Norman, *Anatomy of an Illness*, WW Norton, NY, 1979.

Elkman, *Measuring Facial Movements, Journal of Environmental and Non-verbal Behavior*, 1976, Vol. 1 #1, pages 56-75.

Isen, Alice M., *Positive Affect Facilitates Creative Problem Solving*, Journal of Personality and Social Psychology, June 1987 Vol. 52, #6, pages 1122-1131.

Maclay, Elise, "Vanity," Green Winter—Celebrations of Old Age, Reader's Digest Press 1977

McCormack, Mark H., *What They Don't Teach You At Harvard Business School*, Bantam Books, Toronto: NY, 1984.

McGhee, Paul E., *Humor and Children's Development*, Haworth Press, NY,1989.

O'Connor, Lona, "Working" Column, Detroit Free Press.